T0064453

Ivan's Rules of Management

A Common Sense Approach to Management

Ivan Reynolds MBA

Ivan's Rules of Management

A Common Sense Approach to Management

Ivan Reynolds MBA

PARTRIDGE
A Penguin Random House Company

To order additional copies of this book, contact
Toll Free 800 101 2657 (Singapore)
Toll Free 1 800 81 7340 (Malaysia)
orders.singapore@partridgepublishing.com

www.partridgepublishing.com/singapore

I dedicate this book to Bev.
My Wife, my Partner, my Companion, my Friend, my Support
You have stood by me with unflinching
support and sage advice.
You have shared my ups and downs, victories and defeats.
You have sacrificed you time and life to my career.
You have been a work widow to my long hours either away
at work or during the many years of night time studies.
You have moved from city to city and country to
country, never flinching and never complaining.
I owe my career and success to you!
Thank you
I love you dearly!

"There are three secrets to managing.

The first is to have patience.

The second is to be patient.

And the third most important secret is patience!"

Chuck Tanner

Contents

Work Ethic:

Introduction

My career has been in Logistics. My experiences are based in a logistics background however; management is management whether it is in Administration, Logistics, Production, Manufacturing or anything else. These rules are applicable in any sphere wherein you find yourself in a management or leadership role. Indeed, some of these rules should and could be applied in your private life, to your family and friends and sports colleagues, to social committees and social environments and other place where you interact with other people.

I view these not only as management skills, but indeed, as life skills as well!

My very first job I was more subject to management and discipline than part of it. I learned the discomforts and consequences of non-conformity to the rules and regulations and in some instances the peer admiration for being one of the 'naughty boys'.

I also learned that with such a reputation comes blame for everything whether you were part of it or not. I took a number of lessons out of this which I have learned over the years to apply to my management style. Things like;

- The 'bad boy' is not always as bad as he seems, maybe he is just over exuberant and foolish

- You can jump to a conclusion about someone's behavior, actions, involvement or guilt, but you had better not express an opinion of conclusion until you have thoroughly investigated the facts to the fullest extent
- You can't paint everybody with the same tar brush and expect the same results, personalities will react differently.
- Engage you brain before you engage your mouth so that you don't have to engage reverse gear after you have put your foot in your mouth.
- Know when to stand firm and when to go with the flow.

My second job I converted from being 'the managed' to being 'the manager'. It was a dramatic transition from a communal radio control room environment with no staff responsibilities, no filing or recordkeeping and no residual job responsibilities, to a 24/7 operation with 113 staff members all highly unionised. I was a young very inexperienced white manager in Apartheid South Africa with an all non-white team of what appeared to be mostly militant staff.

On my second day I sat in and observed a disciplinary hearing (which my manager fluffed badly by inadvertently insulting the shop steward) and on the third day I had to hold my first hearing.

The incumbent had been drunk and disorderly while on duty and I meticulously and thoroughly drew up the charges in accordance with the Disciplinary Code & Procedure's guidelines.

I then held the hearing and gave the individual a Written Warning, two Final Warnings and dismissed him twice on the most serious charges.

Flushed with success I then got chewed up and spat out by the Union on a number of cases for procedural reasons. I learned fast and hard that I had to be highly procedural, know the facts, and know the labour law so that cases did not get overturned at a higher level or in labour court or CCMA (Council for Conciliation Mediation & Arbitration) for South Africans. I learned that the very first level of discipline must be able to stand up in court, if not, don't make the decision. I also learned with the help of these shop stewards that corrective action 'outside' the policy and procedure was possible if it was in the interest of the individual. I will explain later. Most of all, I learned that you must be unscrupulously fair, even handed, firm and consistent.

I then made it my business to become expert in policies and procedures and in interpretation of the disciplinary code for all companies I worked for. This stood me in good stead when one of my managers tried to performance manage me out of the company. I was able to defeat the company on procedural grounds despite them having the company legal consultant as prosecutor and HR Director as Chairperson. I was able to leave the company with my reputation intact.

In retrospect, I had been arrogant and headstrong and probably deserved to be fired, but the lesson in this was two-fold. Firstly, know your rules and regulations inside out and stick to them (this to my advantage and their disadvantage).

Secondly, do your homework, prepare properly. They were not prepared as they had assumed they knew everything which they did not.

Lastly, the lesson I took out of this experience was, never assume you know everything or know best, other people know just as much as you if not more. They might do it differently so open your ears, eyes and mind to their suggestions and learn from them.

Over time I have learned to learn from every situation I found myself in. I always ask myself two questions;

1) Firstly, what was the lesson in that?
2) Secondly, is this a good lesson on how to do something, or how not to do something?

Every manager you ever work for will teach you things, some good, some bad. Some things you will want to emulate and apply, some things you would rather forget. It is important to remember the things you would rather forget as a lesson on how not to do something, or how not to treat a person as it is just as important a lesson as how to do so. Always look for the lesson, whether it be negative or positive!

General 'Stormin' Norman Schwarzkopf encapsulated this perfectly where he stated "You learn far more from negative leadership than from positive leadership. Because you learn how not to do it. And, therefore, you learn how to do it"

Negative is also a lesson on how to do something differently and better.

When mentoring junior staff I have found that imparting my experience mostly verbally whilst allowing them to practically apply the lesson, often resulted in information being lost and lessons being forgotten. I then made a list of 'Ivan's Rules of Management' which I would pass on to the incumbent. This list of rules grew over time with my experience.

You will notice that some of them are unorthodox and indeed, could land you in trouble, so discretion is always required when applying them. Ultimately, these rules are the same rules that most everybody else uses, so in fact, they are not really unique or new.

What you will also notice is that many of the rules are integrated with others, similar to others and indeed, the same as others but just from a different perspective.

My foundation of experience was garnered in the South African environment, during and post apartheid. For fourteen years I enjoyed the favorable discriminatory employment policies of the apartheid government that supported and advanced my career. For thirteen years I suffered the discriminatory employment policies of the post-apartheid government that curtailed my advancement and blocked my career. As a consequence of this, I left South Africa and moved to the Middle East.

This turn of events contributed immensely to my development and experience.

The biggest lessons I learned were adaptability and perseverance, 'Adapt or Die' and 'Never Surrender'. No matter how your environment changes, you have to change with it and no matter how difficult things become, never give up, and no matter how old or experienced you are, you are never too old or experienced to learn.

The other major aspect that impacted on my experience is people.I have worked with around 37 different nationalities and a plethora of cultures and religions. The South African environment has been by far the most complex to operate in. The diversity of cultures, the political climate, changing legislation, the climate of self preservation within companies, multiple unions with their own agendas, the air of entitlement and highly competitive companies in a restricted market with a difficult economy all make for a cut-throat workplace.

The environment in the Middle East is far broader with an overarching first world business culture supported by massive third world infrastructure. Discrimination is alive and well but subtle and to some extent expected and tolerated. It is part of the trade-off for working in a tax-free environment where unions are banned and labour exploited but wages far beyond imagination can be earned and the standard of life in the home countries benefits.

Competition is fierce as you have highly qualified and experienced people from all over the world competing for jobs and delivery or dismissal for expatriates is often the driver.

I couldn't have done all of this without a solid educational base. I finished grade 12 of high school and was immediately called up to do two years of military service which included two tours of the operational are. When I left the army I had no direction and took the highest paying job I could find advertised in the newspapers at the time. It was shift work, six days on, one day off which I did for nine years. Having missed my opportunity to go to university, I realised that if I wanted to advance, I had better put some qualifications behind my name. I first studied a Diploma in Road Transportation, a three year course which I did over four years. I then did two years of management studies through a local university Business School, but this was not enough. I then applied for and was accepted to study an MBA. I did the studies in an accelerated program over two years, but it took me a further four years to complete the dissertation as I change jobs three times and moved from South Africa to the Middle East. The dissertation subject was on 'Collaborative Transportation Synergies for Load Optimisation and Cost Reduction on Non-Profitable Routes' sub-titled 'Running with the enemy'. For the dissertation, I set up distribution arrangements between opposition companies both selling chicken into remote locations wherein they shared the transport but competed in the market. It turned out to be a very profitable exercise for both companies as their transportation costs were halved and they could pass the saving on to their customers thus increasing sales.

It is from this mixture of experiences, influences and environments that I emerged and shaped my career, opinions and management ethos.

Hence this book is not only on how to manage subordinates, but indeed, how to manage yourself, your peers, your superiors and your environment.

I have categorized my rules of management into three main categories;

- Personal – How you should behave and act
- Interaction – How you manage others and interact with them
- Work Ethic – How you manage your work

I would like to thank all the managers I have ever reported too for their contribution in my career and development, whether the lessons have been good or bad, they have all been contributory.

Finally, in my second job I received the sagest advice of my career from and old GM. I went to him one day very agitated about a particularly perplexing problem. He studied me briefly; I was about 23 years old and he quietly said to me "Rise above the occasion son!" In other words, do not let the moment drag you down.

Having said all this, you might ask, how I define Management. I define management as the following:

"Management is a continuum of events, activities and actions impacted on and influenced by your actions or reactions on or to them".

Personal:

"The consummate leader cultivates the Moral Law, and strictly adheres to method and discipline; thus it is in his power to control success."

Sun Tzu – The Art of War

1 Always Treat People the way You Want People to Treat You

This is simply a matter of respect and common decency. The people working for you are human beings with feelings, emotions, moods and impressions. They are not slaves, your dog (you shouldn't be treating you dog badly in any case), your servants (shouldn't be treating them badly either) or brainless imbeciles.

The most fundamental desire in any human being is the desire to be recognised and acknowledged. Coupled to this is the desire to be recognised and acknowledged in a respectful manner, to be seen as somebody, a person of some worth. I am sure you the reader have the same desires.

How do you like people to speak to you? With respect, in a mild and friendly manner? With support and encouragement? With recognition for you as a person and for your achievements? I am sure you do. If so, then why do you not apply the same to others?

Everyone wants respect, but respect is something you must earn. You do not gain respect by holding a position with a fancy name and title. People might show respect to the position, but not to the individual occupying that position. If you wish to be respected, you have to first show respect, give respect and act respectfully to others and only then will you earn respect.

Dale Carnegie said that the most important thing to any human being is their name. This is true. Make a point of learning people's names. Do not forget the little people such as the cleaners, tea lady, gardeners etc. They might be people you do not consider as important, but see how quickly you notice just how unimportant they are when your office does not get cleaned or you coffee or tea does not arrive!

All men are borne equal and so equal remain. There are those who believe that they fall into the category describe in George Orwell's Animal Farm of being 'more equal' than others. Do not make this mistake, some people are merely more fortunate than others, hence their elevated station in life. No matter how good or important you think you are, there are always those better and more important than you. If you wish for them to respect you, who are at a lower station than them, then should you not do so to those you consider inferior to you!

The next time you go to the supermarket or restaurant, try addressing the waiter or check-out individual by their name (it's on their name tag, read it). You will be amazed at their response, their smile is more forthcoming, their service more earnest and their desire to please you more pronounced. You will make their day by a simple acknowledgement of their most precious thing, their identity. You might find the next time you go there and should you have the same individual serve you, they remember you (how pleasant it is to be recognised) and acknowledge you and show you a bit more respect than the other customers.

A little respect goes a long way and a smile always brings happy returns, try it.

2 Lead by Word and Deed

There is nothing worse than an empty promise or false commitment. If you say you are going to do something, then you had better do it. If you have set a standard or a requirement, then you had better be the first person to do it or follow it. The quickest way for you to lose the respect of your team is to be a person of empty promises, someone who says things but does not back their words up with action, or someone who lies. As a manager and a leader, you have an obligation to lead from the front, lead in word and deed. You need to be the type of manager who can say to their staff "Do as I do!" Do not be one of those managers who say "Do as I say, not as I do!"

Your team, peers and superiors alike need to be able to trust you and depend on you just like you would like to be able to trust and depend on them. When they ask for assistance, guidance, clarity, commitment or delivery and you commit, then it is imperative that you follow through to the hilt. If you don't, your reputation will be eroded and you will end up sidelined. In other words, if you want to be respected, trusted and depended on, then you first need to deliver on those issues. Treat others as you would like to be treated.

If you manage a warehouse, distribution facility or manufacturing facility and there are specific Personal Protective Equipment (PPE) requirements such as safety shoes, hi-viz vests, helmets, safety glasses etc. you must be the first one to put them on and the last to take them off. The worst example any manager can set is to ignore the company safety requirements because they think they are above the rules.

Often the excuse is, 'I will only be on the floor for a short while!' or 'I know how to be careful" or 'I don't wear that type of stuff'. This shows arrogance and conceit and disrespect for your own company rules and policies, the HSE Officers and personnel, your floor Management and Supervisors responsible for ensuring HSE & PPE compliance and for the staff themselves.

I worked for a construction manufacturing company which had an extensive stockyard for the precast product they manufactured. The HSE PPE requirements amongst other things called for safety helmets to be worn. This was strictly enforced for the labour force by the management who all in turn ignored the requirement and refused to wear them. I could never understand this, did they think their heads were stronger than the labourers heads?

I also worked in the Petrochemicals Industry. Here HSE is of the strictest standards due to the volatile gases and extremely dangerous working environment. Here nobody was exempt from wearing the required PPE, this included the CEO's and the Board of Directors. If they wanted to see the facility, or inspect my warehouse, the full and appropriate PPE was worn or you were simply refused entry.

To lead your team and gain the respect of your team, peers and superiors, you need to be a person of your word; you must walk the talk and lead by word and deed!

Lead from the front where everyone can see what you do, don't be one of those poor managers that stands at the back and shouts at everyone what must be done.

3 Everyone is a Member of the Team, but the Team can only have One Leader

A team works as a cohesive body, each individual playing their interlinking part. You as the 'team leader' are subject to the workings of that team. It is incumbent upon you to be an integral part of the team, but it is also your responsibility to give that team leadership and guidance. Your team can all sing together and play together, but there can be only one conductor, coach, referee, strategist, direction provider, that is you. As leader of the team, you cannot afford to be seen to be favorable or friendly to one person over another. You have to be equally fair, equally strict to everyone. The team will need constant support and encouragement. You need to remind individuals of the importance of their part within the team. There must be clear boundaries for individuals and the team on how they behave within the working environment and indeed in a social environment.

Teamwork will invariably lead to success; a breakdown in team work will invariably lead to failure. Team sports such as soccer or rugby are always such a wonderful analogy of how teams operate. The failure of the individual is the failure of the team and the success of the individual is the success of the team. Each team will have its stars, but each team also has its grafters who form the foundation and platform of that teams success. It is your job as the manager to understand the foibles of each team member and understand how to fire them up. It is your job as the manager of that team to provide leadership both in times of trouble and when things are going well, to direct the team as a whole and manage the individual as an entity.

To build a good team, it is important to develop 'Team Thinking'. You have to learn to think as a team, for the team. You then need to teach your team to think 'Team' as well. The first fundamental of team building is to get the team to understand that there is no 'I' in TEAM, thus all discussions and references where possible must be in the collective or plural. Where possible you need to refer to 'Us' or 'We' and any achievement or failure is 'ours'. By developing a collective mindset, you will strengthen the team as the stronger individuals (whom you need to support) will pull the weaker members with them. You as the Team Leader have to take on the duel responsibility of being both part of the team and leader of the team.

Most of my career I have either worked in a 24/7 operation or managed a 24/7 operation. If like me you find yourself in a 24/7 operation, do not forget the team members who are working the night shift or working over the weekend or on public holidays. There were many nights, weekends and public holidays where I worked with resentment for those lucky people who were at home while I was forgotten. If you have experienced this you will know what I am talking about. I missed many family birthdays, gatherings and functions because I had to work, particularly over days like Christmas. Remember these staff members and if at all possible, pop in to give them a visit. Don't go looking for trouble; just go there to support them and to let them know you haven't forgotten them. In the least a phone call will suffice, but a physical presence will boost morale of the team and garner loyalty to you for the act.

Lastly, no matter how good the team is, it is only as good as its leadership. Manchester United is a good example of that. When Sir Alex Ferguson was the Manager, Man-U were almost invincible. When he left, the same team with the same players suddenly could not perform and went from elite to ordinary in the space of two games.

Be a team player but don't forget to lead the team in the direction your wish to take them

4 I Yam Who I Yam and Dats all I Yam

These are the infamous words of Popeye the sailor man to Olive when she asked him why he couldn't be more like Brutus. You are who you are, don't try and be somebody else. Don't try and play the big executive, the big boss, the wiz-kid or someone or something you are not. Everyone will see right through the charade and your credibility will be undermined or destroyed. Your staff will not respect you, you will be the laughing stock of your peers and senior management will earmark you for sidelining. Nobody likes a smart-arse or someone who is false. Be yourself.

How many times have you heard or said, "That person is so down to earth!"? Do you think the person being referred to is putting up a front, acting down to earth or is it their inner personality shining through? No, this is not a front; they are following Popeye's advice and being who they are.

This is not to say that you must now become chums with everyone on the floor and consider everyone your drinking buddy. As a manager, you still have to maintain a respectable decorum; they must see you as their manager and leader, but someone whom they can approach in times of difficulty for guidance and support.

Your team also needs to see you as someone with a sense of humour, someone who is troubled when things do not go well, but shares their joy and success when they do. They must also see you as someone who will stand firm in the face of adversity, not accept mediocrity as a standard and not afraid to make the hard decisions.

In my opinion, one of the most important virtues a person can have over compassion for others and personal integrity are a good sense of humour and a positive attitude.

One of my strengths and also one of my weaknesses is my sense of humour. I am prone to making quips of a humorous nature in meetings and conversations sometimes where it has not always been appreciated. Humour is not generally appreciated in business, particularly in reports and meetings which are deemed to be matters of serious reflection. Well placed humour can however go a very long way to diffusing a difficult situation or lightening the mood of a boring meeting. I have found it a good means of emphasizing a point on many an occasion. One must however be circumspect when using this tool. Humour must always be neutral, never demeaning or aimed at people or situations where people are negatively impacted. Furthermore, if injecting humour into any report, it must be done in such a manner as to compliment the report as opposed to digress from it. There is a time for humour and that time is never when the situation is grave or serious. Your team must know that you have an good sense of humour, but that you don't find every situation a laughing matter and when you are serious, you mean it.

A lot has been written and said about attitude. Your attitude will dictate both your career path and the direction of your department or division. No matter what the adversity, your team must never see you defeated or negative. This will rub off on them very quickly and your work standards will plummet very quickly. The British expression of 'Keeping a stiff upper lip' particularly in difficult times will sustain you and give your team the confidence to work through and overcome that adversity.

By always exuding a positive can-do attitude, even when you feel the world has collapsed around you, will pull you through nearly every difficult situation. The old adage of 'we'll laugh about this someday' is a good maxim to revert to when all seems lost. Many times in my life when all the calamities of hell seemed to be falling on my head, I have always asked myself the question 'what is the worst that can happen to me? Can I be executed for this?' Thankfully I have never had to say 'yes I can be executed'. If I can't be executed then, there is life, and where there is life there is hope. This is the foundation of positive thinking and a positive attitude. If you have life, you have hope and you can survive. I realise this sounds somewhat dramatic, but I know some of you have been there and understand where I am coming from. There is a difference between being positive and being foolish, positivity is grounded in the realisation that the end has not arrived and you can still turn the situation around. Act positive even when you feel like rubbish inside, it will rub off on others and the results will surprise you.

Ultimately, be yourself, then you don't have to put on an act every day and you won't be caught-out looking stupid trying to be someone that you are not.

5 Be Lavish with you Praise and Hearty with your Approbation

This statement comes from Dr. Norman Vincent Peal in his book 'The Power of Positive Thinking'. Its emphasis is on being positive, nurturing and supportive as opposed to restrictive, negative and aggressive. 'Well how does this help me with my problem staff?' you might ask.

What needs to be added to this statement is 'Be honest in your praise and approbation too!'

If you give people honest feedback while praising them for doing something well, you build a desire in that individual to repeat that action to be able to receive the positive praise again.

Just like you enjoy some praise and approbation for having done something well, be it at work, home, on the sports field or anywhere else, so does you staff.

By identifying the one good thing a problem staff member has done well and focusing on it can go a long way to turning them around. Staff who are perpetually in trouble, perpetually expect trouble and thus attract it. It is your job as manager to identify this trend and to try and break it. If the individual is simply a bad egg, don't waste your time, get rid of them (reg of weg), but most people are not inherently bad; so some hearty and positive feedback will make a huge difference to their self esteem and thus to their attitude to their work.

Do not be false or artificial when praising someone, they will know it and it will generate a bad reaction as opposed to a positive one. When something is wrong, it is wrong, identify it as such and clarify to the staff member why this is and how it can be remedied.

In any counseling session, reprimand or disciplinary action, it is always a good practice to end it on a positive note. Tell the individual that you believe in their ability to improve and do better, that you have confidence in them and will look to seeing them meet their capabilities. Do not tell them that you expect to see them meet your expectations, as this will garner a negative mental reaction, always identify that the achievement is possible within their own capabilities. Be sure that you have this support for them meeting their potential in writing. If it is not put in writing, it will quickly be forgotten, but put it in writing, that individual will go back and reread your positive statement many times.

Follow the Popeye principle when giving people feedback, be who you are and be firm, fair, honest and supportive.

6 Trust

You can't manage without trust, you can't lead without trust and you can't follow without trust.

You trust your management and leadership to make the right decisions, direct you in the right direction, make the right calls and most of all, you trust them to trust you to do the same. You also trust the company to pay you on time, and to deliver the perks and benefits you enjoy as an employee.

Why then is it so difficult to trust the members of your team to do their jobs properly? If you wish to be trusted, you must first be trustworthy. If you wish to be trusted, you must trust in return.

Your team will not always get it right; neither did you in the beginning of your career. That is the reason why you follow up. You follow up not because you don't trust them, but because you do trust them but wish to see if they have achieved the requirements you have stipulated. Dichotomous? Yes indeed it is. The difference in following up with trust or without trust is in your attitude. How you do it and how your team perceives how you do it. It is also in how you react to the findings. If you come across as supportive and guiding, you will have a great response from the individual or team members in question as they will want to please you as well as gain a sense of self satisfaction. However, if you do it in an aggressive, picky demeaning way and pull what they have done to shreds, you will send a very negative message to your team members and break their morale. Managers who are nit-pickers and micro-managers always wonder why they struggle with their teams and why the results in their departments don't always meet their expectations or those of the organisation. It's because they don't trust their teams and thus have to work twice as hard to check on everything that is done themselves.

Managers who trust their teams will generally achieve better results, are less stressed, have more loyalty from their teams (despite there not being a dog), seldom miss a deadline and have a better relationship with their peers.

Trust is a very difficult thing to master, but in all aspects of your life you simply have to let go and trust others to do what they do.

7 Know the Rules, Work the Rules, Stick with the Rules

This is the most fundamentally important requirement in any job you will ever do. Get to know the company's rules, procedures, policies and requirements inside out. Be able to quote the disciplinary procedure from memory. Know the law, country law, labour law, trade law and any other law that could impact you. Know the SOP's, HSE's and ABC's of the company.

Operate strictly within these rules and enforce your staff to do so as well. This way everyone knows exactly where they stand and there can be no deviation or favoritism.

I saw at a very early stage that the unions spent a lot of time and money on training of the shop stewards. They trained them on how to manage a hearing enquiry, company rules and policies country legal legislation affecting their role and so forth. To the contrary, management seldom bothered. Subsequently, the managers did not know the company rules, policies and procedures or the legal ramifications of their actions or decisions as well as the shop stewards did. When it came to staff management and application of the disciplinary code, many managers got caught short and the unions won. This leads to frustration and attempts to get even or to pressurise individual staff members or the union. It becomes a vicious circle of self punishment for the manager because he does not know the rules of the game.

How many times have you heard a manager say 'It's so hard to fire someone!', or indeed, how many times have you said that? Why is this? It is simply because the manager concerned is wishing to take a short-cut, maybe wanting to take an arbitrary decision, or an off-the-cuff decision. The manager is invariably too lazy to work within the framework of the rules at hand. Ouch, you don't like hearing this but in all honesty, is it not perhaps the truth? The manager wants to apply a highly unfair process to the staff member which he\she would not wish applied to them by their manager.

In any disciplinary decision you have to ask yourself the following questions:

- Is this fair?
- Is this in conformance with the company disciplinary policy, rules and regulations?
- Will my actions stand up in court?
- Is this how I would like to be treated?

If you have answered 'yes' to all the questions, then proceed. If you have answered 'no' to anyone of the questions, then do not proceed, review the actions of the staff and what you wish to do.

To dismiss someone is very easy. Just follow the rules and the individual will either fire themselves through repeated wrongful actions, or they will correct their behaviors and your 'problem' will go away.

This entire process goes back to one of my other rules, 'if it's not in writing it never happened'. If you manage your team within the rules and commit to writing what should be committed to writing, you will establish a firm footing and unshakable foundation for the management of your team. You will also have irrefutable evidence when you need it.

If you have acted procedurally and fairly, and everything is documented as it should be, then your decisions will stand in any Court.

Lastly, never lose sight of the fact that you are dealing with people, whilst operating within the rules you still need to apply a modicum of humanity to your process and decisions.

This applies as much to you as it does to the individual staff member. You as the leader must set the example to your staff by always adhering to the company rules.

Starting and finishing times, lunch and tea breaks, HSE and PPE rules and regulations or dress codes. These rules, policies and procedures have all been developed and introduced for a reason. You as the individual need to adhere to them or you yourself might fall foul of the rules. As manager, leader or employee, it is imperative that you set the example and comply implicitly. You are not above the law so should not act as if you are. Should you see your peers or seniors breaking the rules, it is incumbent upon you to bring it to their attention, particularly in a working environment such as a production facility or a warehouse. You might upset some people, but you will gain an immense amount of respect from your staff if they see you challenging people transgressing the company's procedures. This in turn will make it easier for you to enforce and your staff more willing to comply.

Don't learn the harsh lesson of short-cuts and impatience, take time to operate within the rules and you will seldom experience problems.

This applies in any company or country you might work in.

8 Share the Wealth

So you have achieved the position you now hold through hard work, many committed hours, difficult studies and education and many lessons learned both good and bad along the way. You deserve to be where you are. Well done!!

So what to do now? That is the question!

You need to reflect on how hard you have worked, how many hours sacrificed to studies and all the many nights and weekends sacrificed along the way. But most importantly, you need to remember the people who helped to get to where you are now. Family who have supported and encouraged you, teachers and lecturers who have both berated you and encouraged you and imbued you with the technical and strategic knowledge you have been able to use. And what about the managers and colleagues who have helped you with words of encouragement, shown you how to do things, how to achieve results, motivated you, given you a break and boost into greater responsibility and have shown their faith and trust in you.

How do you repay all these people?

It is quite simple, you share the wealth. You share the wealth of your knowledge, education, experience and training with your peers and subordinates. You mentor individuals who you have identified as having great potential, you provide training to your leadership team on how to manage people and situations and you share your experiences with your peers who you see are struggling.

It is important to give back some of what you know for this will imbue you with a great sense of satisfaction and enhance your reputation amongst your peers and colleagues and generate great respect for you from your team.

The old adage of 'It's better to give than to receive' will be truly understood once you start sharing your knowledge.

You will also learn the old adage of 'you will reap what you sow'. In sharing your experience and knowledge with others, you will find people open up to you; they listen to you and will show you respect and cooperation you never imagined you could experience. It is truly a self fulfilling circle.

Just a mild warning; do not fall into the trap of becoming Mr. Professor Know It All. Do not impose yourself on others. Offer them what you have and allow then to take it for them self. You can take a horse (or camel) to water, but you can't make it drink, it must choose to do so itself.

Remember Popeye's lesson, be who you are. People will be more open to learning from you if you remain humble and down to earth.

9 Do Your Homework

There are a number of expressions that support this statement such as 'Failing to plan is planning to fail' and 'Fore warned is fore armed' etc. What do they mean?

My father used to always say, 'Do your homework so that you know what you are dealing with'. When a failure was witnessed, sometimes on TV or with one of the family, he would simply say 'They\you haven't done their/your homework'.

Do not leave things up to chance, do not assume and do not take for granted for these actions and attitudes will always lead to failure. Do you homework, investigate, research, interrogate, follow up, gather data, information or anything that can be used to assist you with your action.

Too many times in my experience, team members have come to me with a long face and a sad story about something that went wrong and in the analysis it comes out that they did not do their homework on the subject. They were therefore ill prepared for what transpired once the wheels of action had been set in motion. It is as simple as school, when you didn't do your homework, you had problems, sometimes not immediately, sometimes at a later stage compounded.

When investigating an accident or incident or a disciplinary infringement, do a thorough investigation of all the evidence provided. Do not get caught up in the emotion of the situation and do not take all that has been said at face value. Always ask the question 'why'. Why did it happen, why did he do it, why do they say so. Question the evidence until you cannot ask any more questions. By testing the evidence thoroughly you will uncover not only the reasons why it happened, but the root cause of the issue. Once you have the root cause you can put all the evidence together and formulate an unbiased factual set of evidence to the issue.

Be prepared and do everything in your power to ensure you have covered all bases in your preparation. Do your homework.

10 Now is the future, but tomorrow is another day

Life is full of dichotomies and work is one of them. Why do we work so hard? We do this in the hope of achieving recognition by our management. This recognition will then hopefully result in promotion and advancement which will result in more money, authority and recognition. But it is not easy to achieve this recognition because in any working environment, there is so much to do, and when you have done it, there is still so much more to do and everything is urgent and should have been done yesterday. But ask yourself this question; is what you are trying to finish critical to the operation? Is it critical to the company's financial position? Is it critical to immediate customer satisfaction? Or, can it wait until tomorrow, for tomorrow is another day and believe me, the operation will trundle on whether you finish the report or not, or complete the task or not.

I have always asked myself the question, 'If I die on the way home tonight, will this unfinished report result in the failure of the company or the total disgrace of my name and reputation, would anyone miss it or even care and invariably, the answer is 'No'.

There is always a tomorrow and tomorrow will always come. Some things no matter how important they seem to you from your position can wait until tomorrow. Try and see this urgent thing you just have to get done from a global perspective of the whole operation or indeed the business, and you will notice that it is quiet probably somewhat insignificant and the world will not come to an end if you do not finish it. Besides, when you come in tomorrow, you will be refreshed, rested and have the zeal to tackle the task or report with enthusiasm and in all probability do a much better job of it than had you forced through under duress the night before.

Having said that, do not fall into the procrastination trap. Procrastination is the thief of time. If you can do it today, then do it.

11 Don't forget the reason why you are doing all this

Have you ever sat and wondered "Why am I doing all this?" Of course you have. You come to work every day to build your career, soar with the eagles and build security for your future, family, and hopefully make plenty of money. You want to be able to buy a nice house, a good car for yourself and one for your partner. You want to be able to send your children to a good school and ultimately a good university. You want to be able to cover all medical bills, food bills, clothing, leisure and sporting activities for yourself and the kids. You want to be able to afford holidays and everything else and still have money left over.

So you work, long and hard hours, trying to just finish this report, or that task or some other thing that must get done, and you sacrifice your life, your family, your children, your pets and your leisure time to the great God work in hopes of a better financial return to be able to afford all the lovely things you want.

The consequence of this is your partner only sees you late at night when you are exhausted and your relationship suffers. Your children grow up with an absent parent who is never there to help with homework, never attending their sporting and extramural activities, never providing guidance and discipline or just being there to give them love and hugs.

And you, you suffer from overwork, stress, heart conditions, high blood pressure, overweight, diabetes, you smoke too much and drink too much. You find you cannot relate to these strange things called teenagers in your house with bad attitudes and drug problems or your partner who has carved out a new life for themselves.

Yes, you have forgotten the reason why you work so hard - your family. You are not indispensible to the company and nothing is so critical at work that you must sacrifice your family.

General Charles De Gaulle, leader of the French resistance in WW II and President of the French Republic once said "The graveyards are full of indispensible men!"

You have to have a balance, there is nothing wrong with working hard and long hours sometimes, but this must be the exception to the rule. Tomorrow is another day, your work will still be there waiting for you like an overly needy lover, but you children will grow up and away from you.

Finish up, go home, spend the weekend with the kids and attend their plays and sporting activities. Give your partner the 'You' they fell in love with and committed to spending their life with. Take some time to love your pets, play with the dog, groom the cat, ride your horses, or go fishing.

Select activities that include your family. Relaxing by playing golf for instance is only beneficial if your whole family plays golf, if not you are now converting your family from work widows and orphans to golf widows and orphans. No I don't have anything against golf; I am just using it as an example!

You must balance you work, home and social life. Failure to do so will result in something having to give, and often the first thing to give is your family.

Do not sacrifice them on the great altar of work in hopes of blessing them. You cannot do both!

12 Close off the Week and Start Afresh

As a young operations manager, I had a GM who could really ride my case. He was hard and everything had to be perfect. Invariably by the end of the week I hated him with all my might and just wanted to escape home for the weekend. But it was not that easy. I would not sneak away from work early on a Friday as a point of principle. It has never been one of my practices as this sets an extremely poor example for your staff. I would wait for 16h30 to come so that I could leave.

This GM had a small well stock bar fridge in his office. On a Friday afternoon between 16h00 and 16h30 he would call his management team in for a drink before the close of the week. Invariably it was one or perhaps two drinks and then everyone left for home. This was strictly managed to ensure nobody was over the alcohol consumption limit when driving home.

He was also well aware of how hard he had pushed me and so I would get the inevitable phone call "Reynolds, stop sulking and come and have a drink!" It was more of an instruction than a request and whilst I could refuse, it would have been most rude and un-courteous to do so. I would then reluctantly leave my office in the middle of the warehouse and trudge upstairs to his office. The beer was always cold. He would always hand me the first beer and say, "Here, have that, you deserve it!" No business was allowed to be discussed and everyone would just unwind.

The lessons I learned from this were numerous. This GM was the individual most responsible for infusing a strong and ethical management foundation in me of all managers I reported too. I learned principles of management, warehouse and cold chain management and attention to detail amongst other things. But the lesson most valuable was never to leave your staff for the weekend without having made amends for the weeks work and pressure. To close the week on a positive neutral note, leave it behind and come back the following week to start afresh.

It is important that neither you, nor your staff come in at the beginning of the week carrying residual hard feelings and animosity from the previous week. Such feelings tend to fester and break down the relationship and work performance and must be left in the past where it belongs.

Do not interpret this as a 'forgive all sins' exercise wherein someone's serious discretions or poor performance is all forgotten. Indeed, it is not and these things will still need to be managed, but even the malcontents, lazy or trouble causers do something right in the course of their duties. Focus on that as the 'pick-me-up' to close off the week i.e. 'Well done on that report', or 'thank you for the effort in resolving that operational issue' etc. You will find that some of your so called 'problem children' will respond positively to the smallest approbation or praise and turn over a new leaf.

It is important for you as well as your team to know that despite all that has transpired, there is a re-set button to start afresh. A little word of encouragement just before someone goes home can be powerful in building your team relations.

It will also recharge your team members for the coming week by lifting their spirits when they go home for the weekend.

So, always clear the decks and leave the negative behind so that a fresh and positive start can be made at the opening of the new week

13 Management by Walk-About

The best way to know what is happening in the environment you manage is to go and have a physical look-see for yourself. Managing a production facility, warehouse or distribution center or any other facility, you should start every day with a quick walk around the place. There is nothing so urgent that it can't wait. If it has waited overnight for you to get in to work, it can wait a further twenty or forty minutes while you tour the facility that you are in charge of. If you are too busy to take time out to walk through your facility, then quite simply, you are not coping with the job, resign and find an easier job. Harsh words? Yes indeed, but the truth. To get your finger on the pulse of the state of hygiene, HSE application and compliance, staff morale and motivation, stock levels, state of the materials handling equipment, state of inbound, binning and picking operations and everything else that is happening, you have to be there to see for yourself. Engage your staff in discussion, look at what is happening and identify problems and improvement opportunities. Listen to what they have to say, yes, there will be a lot of moaning and complaining at times, but it will give you an indication into the health of the operation and the morale of your staff.

You can't always rely on feedback from your supervisors and managers. It is not that you don't trust them, but no matter how good they are, they will only tell you either what they want you to know, what they think you want to hear or part of the story. It is the natural instinct of self preservation, just like you give filtered information to your manager and superior. Take note of the body language of the staff from the lowest level to the most senior person in your team. Are they relaxed? Do they smile a lot and easily? Are they comfortable in engaging in conversation or answering questions? Are they bold or furtive in their actions and mannerisms?

These indicators will tell you what the morale of the team is and consequently, what out-put and productivity you can expect from them.

So don't be a 'Soft Shoes' Manager or an 'Armchair 'Manager. If you want to know what is happening in your operation, get off your butt and get out onto the floor.

This also applies if you manage an office environment. You ask "What is there to look at in an office environment?" There is plenty, observe how your staff are interacting, is there harmony or tension (maybe you need to shuffle some desks around), are the ergonomics good, flow unrestricted, do the staff have enough space to work in, is it neat and tidy, what risks and hazards are there, etc, etc, etc.

Last but not least, walking around your operation allows you time to think and to contemplate issues and problems or find solutions. Take someone with you on a training walk and get some fresh air and exercise.

The benefits of a daily walk-about can never be underestimated, get moving!

14 Sometimes You Just Have to Blow Your Own Trumpet

Sometimes a beautiful flower in a pot standing against the wall will simply go unnoticed by people in the garden. Why is this? It is simple; it has done nothing to draw attention to itself. It needs to put out a lovely scent to bring to the passer by's attention its beauty. This is particularly pertinent if it is a small flower, or if it is in an obscure position.

We are sometimes guilty of the same thing, being obscure. One works hard, delivers the results and then watches the office loud-mouth get all the accolades and promotions. This is invariably because you have not advertised your achievement in the right manner or forum. It is fine and good to submit your reports, statistics and KPI's but if you don't talk to key persons about these results and achievements, they might never know they were your work. There is a big difference between boasting about your achievements and raising them in discussion with others, particularly management. Also, do not approach people in an obsequious manner with a wringing of the hands and cowering of the head as they might just dismiss you as someone sucking up for something or looking for brownie points. Present yourself with confidence and assurance but humbly and your will be noticed.

You need to target your audience. Speak to people to whom your achievements matter or have contributed. Many people find this hard to do. They don't like the lime-light, don't want to draw attention to themselves, don't want to look forward or aggressive and don't want to 'push' themselves in front of their colleagues. They will pay the price for this.

Sometimes, as they say, 'you gotta do what you gotta do!". How often have you heard people in discussion saying "He was such a great guy!", "She was such a hard worker!" after someone has already left and invariably surprise the whole office when resigning because they seemed part of the furniture. Had these people perhaps blown their own trumpet, advertised themselves a bit, they might have received the promotion they were looking for, or the recognition they needed, but by remaining quiet, they were overlooked and they then left – unhappy and unfulfilled and with a weakened CV.

Just be sure that when you blow your own trumpet you can walk the talk and back up your claims with facts.

So, don't be afraid to blow your own trumpet, otherwise all you might hear is the last post!

15 Having done all, stand firm

There comes a time in everyone's life and in every operation and in every project where you have done all that you can do.

You might not be comfortable with the results or the achievement, or you might be worried about the reaction of those who will inspect/visit/audit, but if you have done all that you can do, then this is the time to stand firm. Once you have climbed to the top of the hill, then you must stop or you will start climbing down the other side.

Faffing around like a chicken scratching for grubs will not change the situation. If what you can do will not have a fundamental and positive impact on the result or presentation, then leave it as is and stand firm.

Present your work with confidence and be open to criticism for improvement.

This is part of life's learning curve. Most importantly, have faith in yourself and your abilities!

Interaction:

"Never tell people how to do things. Tell them what to do and they will surprise your with their ingenuity."

General George Patton

16 Explain as if to a little child

I got this bit of wisdom out of Readers Digest somewhere back in the 1980's. I took note of it and it has proven to be a very valuable piece of advice. I have been fortunate in life that my first language is English and I went to a school that taught good English (although my mother might not always agree). I have always operated in a multi-cultural environment. I have nearly always had colleagues of at least three different cultural and language backgrounds, and operations where the staff have been from anywhere between two and seven different ethnic and cultural groups and thus language backgrounds.

Clear concise and to the point explanations or instructions are critical. To do this, keep your sentences short and to the point. Try and bullet-point the explanation to some extent, but do not make the points so short as to become cryptic and ambiguous. Explain as if you are explaining to a child, but do not be condescending and insulting in how you do this.

Do not make the mistake of asking people if they understand, of course they are going to say yes, nobody likes to look stupid. Rather ask them to repeat back to you what you have explained and then ask clarifying questions so that you know that they clearly understand what you are talking about.

Pronunciation is very important. Different cultures have different pronunciations for words that might differ drastically from yours. I worked for a construction company in the Middle

East. When I joined them, as Transport Manager I was required to attend the weekly construction progress meeting where every project was reported on in detail. In this meeting there were a plethora of nationalities including Danish, Lithuanian, Finish, South African English, South African Afrikaner, Indians, Pakistanis, Philippines, Indonesians, Swedes and so forth. The first meeting I attended I thought I was losing my mind. I sat there for four hours and could only understand what was been said by the South Africans. Everyone was speaking English, but with the plethora of accents, pronunciation deviations, means of expression, I was simply unable to attune my ear to the differences. Upon walking out of the meeting I said to one of the old hand South Africans that I thought I was going nuts as I hadn't understood a single word of the proceedings. He merely chuckled and said "You will get used to it". I did and I was able to pass that advice on to newcomers.

The lesson here was that firstly, one must listen carefully and attune one's ear to the accents of others and what is being said, be patient when listening and secondly, explain in such a manner as to be sure that what you have said is clear and understood by all.

Remember, to people of other nationalities, you have a funny accent and are difficult to understand. Western, Eastern, Middle Eastern, Far Eastern and African cultures are all radically different and therefore what is important, what is understood and how it is said all vary considerably. You must listen very clearly so that you first can understand. Do not become impatient with someone from another culture who is struggling to make themselves understood. Take the time to listen and if you do become impatient, take a moment to reflect what it would be like for you to have to speak that individual's language.

Take the time to make sure everyone is very clear on what is being said and meant and you will have a productive and generally happy environment for you and your team.

Listen carefully and explain as if to a little child.

17 Follow-up, Follow-up, Follow-up

The biggest failure of any supervisor or manager is the failure to follow-up. How many times have you ended up in a difficult or embarrassing situation with your seniors or a client for something you were supposed to do that you delegated and it was not done properly. In theory it should have only been once or twice, unless you are a slow learner.

People are fallible, but managers are not supposed to be fallible, that is why you have to follow-up. After issuing any instruction, request, or directive (clearly in writing), you must follow-up to see that it has been done as required. This follow-up can be by means of a phone call, 'Hello, how did that task go that I assigned you? Please send it to me so that I can have a look at it!' You might need to get up from your desk and get out of your office and take a walk to the location of the task to inspect it insitu.

In my second job I was managed by a little old grey haired man with a thin grey moustache. He was general manager and everyone was deathly afraid of him. You did not go to his office for anything if you could help it, but should you have to go, or if you were summonsed, then you had better have all your facts in a row and a notepad and a pen to take notes with. He had a reputation for having the memory of an elephant. If he asked you to provide him with a report, or some data, on a certain day in the future at a particular time, you had better be there with it on time or you would receive a dreaded phone call from him at the appointed time. I was curious as to how he remembered all these things so far into the future considering that I had a memory like a bucket without a bottom in it. (For the youngsters, this was in a time and distant past, before the advent of the desk-top computer, or lap-top computer, even before the time of mobile phones or smart phones – yes, there was a time before mobile phones). On one of my visits to his office I summed up the courage and asked him what his secret was. I was astounded by the simplicity of his system. He would diarise it in his diary. Seems logical, even simplistic, but to a junior and inexperienced staffer it was a revelation. To this day I keep a diary (the book type) on my desk wherein I record future events, to do lists, deadlines and delivery expectations for myself and for my staff.

The lesson here is that you do not need a complex complicated system to track everything you need to follow-up on. Whatever method you use, the important thing is to follow-up. Remember to place your observations on your follow-up in writing to the incumbent so that they are crystal clear of your impressions and any comments or instructions that followed.

Failure to follow-up is failure to execute.

18 Reg of Weg – If the people don't want to change, change the people.

I worked in a leading company in South Africa where one of the directors had the expression 'Reg of Weg'. This translated from Afrikaans means 'Right or Gone'. There is only one way to do something - that is the correct way. This naturally applies to you first as the manager.

Each member of you team should have a clearly defined job profile or job description with clearly outlined and stated KPI's (Key Performance Indicators) or KPA's (Key Performance Areas). Each member of your team must be properly and thoroughly trained in the execution of their task. Then each member of your team must be expected to deliver against their KPI's or KPA's and they must be held accountable for any failure or non-conformance. If necessary, re-train, then council to afford them the opportunity to rectify their shortfall in performance and delivery.

However, if a staff member does not want to change, then change the staff member. It is that simple. You as the manager will be held accountable for your team's failures. It is highly unprofessional and simply cowardly to blame them for any failure when confronted about it if you have not taken every step necessary to either bring their performance in line or to replace them if they haven't responded accordingly.

This links in firmly with knowing the rules and also engaging the shop stewards. If the individual has been counseled with the shop stewards present, and they are now aware that progressive discipline is taking place, they will be obliged to apply more pressure on the individual to comply as their position is now more difficult in resisting management. Don't forget however, that any interaction with the union is in fact a team effort.

If it is a direct reportee, you need to run the counseling, performance management and disciplinary processes with the assistance and physical presence of HR on all occasions.

These are what are referred to as the 'tough decisions'. It is tough to have to dismiss a person knowing that your decision is impacting on the lives of that member's family and children. It is even tougher when you know that the individual is simply obstinate, difficult or obstructive, however, if that individual wishes to sacrifice their family for a position stance or attitude, then the responsibility for the consequences are on their head, not yours. It sometimes helps to explain this to the individual, but in my experience, not always.

19 OK is not good enough

How may time have you been feeling depressed, or slightly ill, over tired or simply off colour and someone has asked you "How are you?" and you have replied, "I'm ok!". You are not good, not well, not fine, not feeling great, not on top of the world, you are lying to cover up how you really feel, in fact, it is just too much effort to explain how you really are feeling.

How many times have you asked someone, perhaps one of your children how an experience was and they responded "It was ok!" and you can see the disappointment in their face and hear it in their voice.

The same applies to standards in operations, ok means it is not good, not great, not excellent, not the best, it is below what you are expecting it to be.

If you are not prepared to accept 'ok' as acceptable, then why should you feel that delivering 'ok' is fine?

If something is not worth doing properly, or if it is not worth doing too the best of your ability, then it is simply not worth doing at all. Jedi Master Yoda in 'The Empire Strikes Back' put it simply, "Do or do not, there is no try!"

This also counts for something you really do not wish to do but have too, or are not interested in doing but need too. The means and standards, to which you do things, perform tasks, deliver service or products all allude to your personal standards of excellence. You will be judged by what standards you deliver and by what quality you deliver.

So only the best is ok, for ok is simply not good enough!

20 The Shop Stewards and the Union can be Your Best Friend

Unions and shop stewards are a fact of life, love em or hate em, they are there. Shop stewards have a job to do. Their job is to protect their members (your team) from management exploitation, unfair labour practices, discrimination etc. Their job is to ensure the welfare of their members.

You job as a manager is to look after your staff, ensure they have a safe and healthy working environment to work in, ensure their needs are met, that they are looked after and that they perform in harmony with the other members of the team in order to deliver the required results.

So you and the shop stewards have the same job when it comes to the welfare of the staff it seems. Indeed, you are on the same team.

Engage the Union and involve the shop stewards in the 'management' of the team. If you have an individual who is not performing, or is misbehaving, or malfunctioning, bring the shop stewards in and have a counseling session with the individual. Make it clear to the shop steward that you place as much responsibility on him to help correct the staff member's problems as you do; for if the matter should escalate to a disciplinary hearing, your will ask him to account to the hearing on what he has done to assist the individual. In addition, he will be asked by the individual's family members and possibly work colleagues why he did not stop the individual from the actions that led to his demise if he knew about them. As shop steward, he is obliged to fight you tooth and nail in defense of the individual and if he does not, he is not doing his job. Do not criticize or attack the shop stewards for doing their job. What it will do, is give the shop steward impetus in addressing the actions of the individual.

In time, trust in your fairness will be built and you will be in a position to try some radical or drastic measures "off the record" with the support of the shop steward if it can lead to rehabilitation of the individual and in saving his job.

I managed a particular youngster in the 80's who came from a broken home, lived with his grandmother and grew up in one of the most gang and drug infested suburbs of the Cape Flats in Cape Town. He was a kid looking for a way to jail. His elder brother also worked for me and a more stable hardworking family man you couldn't find anywhere. They like many brothers were like chalk and cheese. Mark (for that was his name, selected from the Holy Bible by his mother (as was his brother's name Hiram) was around nineteen years of age and had been walking a fine line on the wrong side of the rules. It came to pass that he for the third (and final) time was appearing before me on disciplinary charges. The shop steward representing him was a very religious man and like a father to many of the staff. I took the hearing to the conclusion but then put the verdict in abeyance. I then said to Mark, "I have tried to save your job but you are determined to lose it, if I cannot save your job, at least I can try and save your soul!" This had the shop steward sitting bolt upright in his chair as this was highly un-procedural. I then asked the shop steward if he would support me in one last attempt to bring back this wayward lad onto the straight and narrow. He with some suspicion agreed. I then told Mark that as his name was Mark, he was to read one chapter from the book of Mark in the New Testament every evening. He was then to report to me the next morning with the shop steward in question and explain what he had read. I would also read the chapter in question and so would the shop steward. Hopefully he would learn something that would help him from becoming a lost soul and a police statistic. The shop steward thought this was a wonderful idea. The very next morning I had Mark brought to me (he had tried to dodge me). When asked, he said that he had forgotten to read the first chapter. I simply took a bible out of my desk drawer and gave it to him and asked the shop steward to take him to the staff canteen and ensure he read the chapter and then bring him back to me. This the shop steward did with great enthusiasm and with great humiliation to Mark as he was suddenly the laughing stock of the entire workforce. The end result was that he read the entire book of Mark and discussed it with the shop steward and I one chapter at a time. He also never got into trouble again and after staying with the company for a further five or so years left and joined the Police Force.

In another instance with the same Shop Steward, I had a youngster learn the whole of Psalm 121, one verse per day. Each morning before commencing shift he had to come to my office with the Shop Steward and recite the psalm from the beginning to where he had learned. He also turned over a new leaf. I would like to believe that these two youngsters had 'seen the light', but I think the 'corrective' action was much more painful and they did not want to have to go through that again.

A final example was a middle-aged driver who had just suffered a divorce and had lost the will to be part of society. He had an unblemished work record until this occurred and he simply started turning up for work late or not turn up at all. We raced through the three formal disciplinary stages and I found myself with a person who if I dismissed him, would probably end up in the gutters literally. I was extremely worried and had discussed this man's case with the Shop Stewards on numerous occasions. Despite their efforts at counseling him and my efforts, nothing had worked and we had reached the end of the road. Again in the hearing, I departed from procedure and set the verdict and final sanction in abeyance. The individual's name was Pool and I said to him in a last ditched effort to save his job, "Mr. Pool, whilst you offence does not merit dismissal, procedurally we have no option. I do feel however that your behavior has been that of a school child and I believe I need to punish you like a school child!" This naturally had the two Shop Stewards sitting upright with ears pricked. I then instructed Mr. Pool that he was to write out 1000 lines to the effect of 'I must inform my Supervisor if I am not coming to work'. The hearing was on a Monday and I gave him until the Friday to complete the lines. When Friday morning arrived, there were no lines from Mr. Pool and it looked as if I would have to re-open the hearing and dismiss him. However, it was Friday and staff were paid weekly. I had his pay packet brought to me and had him brought to me with the Shop Steward. It was 11h00 and I ask where the lines were. Mr. Pool responded that he had not done them yet. I told him that he had until 16h30 that day to get the lines to me. If he failed, then I would hold his pay packet for the weekend and he could collect it when he had finished. This horrified him as he depended on the pay packet but he knew I was serious. I gave him a new notepad and three pens for the task.

At 16h25 he was bundled into my office by the Shop Steward. His right hand was completely cramped and he was unable to hold anything in it, but in his left hand he held the notepad. I was amazed but also pleased. I made a big show of checking every single page, he had numbered the lines, and the script had gone through several metamorphoses as he forgot what to write and changed it. There was evidence of where he had tried to hold two pens at the same time and where he had written with his left hand when his right failed. The last page was illegible, but there were 1000 lines submitted on time. The consequence of this exercise was that M. Pool never missed a day's work, never came late and never transgressed any of the rules for the remainder of the time I worked there. The hearing is still in abeyance. I gave him his pay packet which he gracefully accepted.

The lessons here are that it is your responsibility as manager to fight just as hard to save an employee's job as it is the Union's and that in order to be able to take radical action, you will need the support of the Shop Stewards

Building trust and a working relationship with the union can go a long way to making your life as a manager easier. To achieve this you first have to show that you care.

As Bear Grylls, survival expert, adventurer and writer quoted he was taught during his military training "People don't care how much you know until they know how much you care!"

21 Dealing with Diversity and Dissent

Isn't it wonderful when you have a team of harmonious workers who all get along and nobody ever argues with you? Whatever you ask gets done, whatever you instruct is carried out by willing staff and everyone agrees with everything you say.

But there is always that one damn staff member who has to question everything you say, argues with everyone and is never in agreement with you or the rest of the team. The bad egg!

So you think it's time to get rid of them, clean house, re-harmonise the team – bad mistake!

Are you a manager or autocrat, leader or dictator? Dictators and autocrats manage their teams by eradicating anyone that is not in agreement with them, Adolph Hitler, Joseph Stalin and Saddam Hussain are good examples of this. Is your management or leadership style akin to theirs?

In any good team there must be a balance. People who agree and those who question. The individual you have labeled the bad egg, is it that they are really bad and disruptive or do they just like to question everything, seek clarity on anything they are not sure of, or like to first explore alternatives. People like this can add value to your team. They will uncover the flaws in any plan or strategy put forward. They will highlight the 'hidden pitfalls' that nobody else though of and that could sink you project.

These individuals you need to develop and encourage. I say develop because their ability to think laterally and out of the box needs to be managed in the context of what you are trying to achieve. Give them the leeway and latitude they crave but direct it in a positive direction. Ask them for alternatives to your plan based on their argument. It is not good enough just to object, it must be done constructively and with a solution in mind. Allow their diversity to be channeled in a positive and constructive direction. Take a look at yourself, maybe you are one of these people that someone channeled and directed in the right direction and you are now reaping the benefits through your appointment to a leadership position.

What is the difference between diversity and dissent in a team setting? It is quite simple, diversity in a person is an attitude that can be managed and directed to a positive outcome; dissent is an attitude that resists direction, remains negative and cannot be directed to a positive outcome.

Dissenting individuals tend to be disruptive, break down moral and disrupt the harmonious flow of your team. They are toxic people who disagree for the sake of disagreeing, do not comply with requirements and generally do not work with the team. Sometimes these individuals have an ingrained grievance which is the root of their dissenting attitude and if you can uncover that and address it you can turn the individual around. Many of them do not want to be turned around for they are happiest when unhappy and they must simply go.

The big difficulty is how to deal with these individuals. This will take a process of counseling to try and rectify the individuals behavior, and if that does not work, progressive disciplinary action. This is where all your skills as a manager and leader have to come together:

- First, treat the individual as you would like to be treated but you must also be direct, honest and clear in your communications. Everything must be communicated very clearly and concisely in writing outlining the actions, the requirements, the discussions, the agreements and the deadlines. Remember, if it is not in writing, it never happened!
- Second, know the rules, work within the rules, stick to the rules. In a case like this you first want to correct the behavior of the individual to keep them as a positive contributing member of the organisation and to protect them and their family from their own bad actions. If this doesn't work, then you need to work the person out of the position perhaps into another environment more suited to them within the organisation, or if necessary, work them out of the company. You must work within the rules and strictly within the rules. If the rules are unclear and ambiguous, then err on the side of caution and fairness. Treat them the way you would like to be treated if you were in their position. Work closely with HR, but be careful, I have known many an HR Manager to be a puppet of senior management or power hungry and to take actions both unfair and

illegal. Work strictly within the procedures so that if the individual takes the company to labour court, that your procedural application is impeachable. Then your fairness must follow suit in being unquestionable.

- Third, ensure that you have done your homework on this case. That it has been investigated thoroughly, that the evidence is available, and irrefutable. Do not get into a 'He says, she says' situation where one person's word without proof or supporting facts is used. It won't stand up in court. So know the facts, have the facts at hand and be able to present the facts in a consecutive constructive and clear manner.
- Forth, if the individual is a member of a union, have you engaged the union shop stewards in an attempt to rectify the recalcitrant behavior from the beginning? If not, go back to the start and work with the union to try and change the individual's behavior, it is the fair thing to do. If you have engaged the union from the start, then proceed as normal. Beware of pleas for clemency from the union, if you step outside of the rules you could be setting a precedent for future cases.
- Fifth, having done all, clear your conscience and stand firm in your decision. Fire them.

Diversity is a positive attribute that can be manipulated and managed for the good of the individual and the good of the team. Dissent is both toxic and contagious and must be eradicated as soon as possible.

22 Friends in the Work Place

This I believe is one of the most difficult things to have to deal with as a manager. What is the fundamental difference between a friend and colleague or employee? The distinction between the three can quickly become a blurred and grey area if you as the manager are not vigilant.

You must be able to treat you friends like staff and colleagues while at work and revert to being friends outside of the work arena. Likewise, your friends need to accept that this is the status quo and not expect special favours from your because your are their friend. If your friendship should fail as a result of this requirement, then your friend was not such a good friend after all. A good friend should respect the fact that in the workplace you are not friends but co-workers or possibly superior/subordinates. If you do not manage your friend the same as you do the rest of your team, two things will happen;

- You will lose the respect and loyalty of your team as you have become untrustworthy.
- You will have to take responsibility and blame for any failure on behalf of your friend's actions or inactions.

I have worked with friends both as superiors and subordinates. As a subordinate for me it was easy, I respected my friend so I accepted him as my superior and submitted myself as a subordinate staff member and nothing more. I also ensured that I delivered excellence or the very best that I could so that I did not place my friend in a difficult position.

As a superior it was a lot more difficult. My one friend respected me in the same manner as I did in the above description and delivered against requirement. I had no problem with her and the working relationship worked well and our friendship stood the test of time.

Another friend I had was in a key operational position which he approached with a very lax attitude. It was an extremely difficult situation and I failed to address the matter correctly which heaped tons of trouble on my head. I felt that I could not refer the operational failures to him as I had not addressed them with him correctly and thus had to carry the can for the failure myself. I was in a relatively senior position and this turned out to be damaging to my career. My friend did not try and take advantage of me in any way; I simply did not manage him correctly. He to this day is not aware of the problems his relaxed attitude and failure to deliver caused me. It was a harsh lesson well learned hence my warning to you. You could be sacrificing your career for your maligned friendship, or you could be jeopardizing your friend's career through your failure to address the issue or your expectations of special treatment.

I learned a harsh lesson as a youngster in boarding school. It was my first year in boarding school in grade eight. My brother, then in grade twelve was a prefect in my hostel and was in charge of one of the dormitories. I thought it would be a good idea to move into his dormitory to be closer to him. He was then and still is to this day a man of high moral and ethical integrity. After lights out at night nobody was allowed to talk.

I soon found out that if anyone talked, the culprits and I always got called into my brother's office cubicle and I was punished with them. This punishment consisted of two or three blows on your backside with a cane that he retained just for that purpose. I questioned this of him and he simply told me that in order to ensure nobody thought he was favouring me simply because I was his brother; he included me in the punishment. It was not malicious but indeed a safety feature to prevent me from being bullied by others if he did favour me. Needless to say, I moved out to another safer dormitory where if I was punished, at least I had earned it.

I have remembered this painful lesson of love and ethics and respect my brother for having taught me this important life lesson. There is no place in business or profession for nepotism or favour.

If you find yourself in a situation where you have friends in the work place, either peers, senior or subordinates, take the time out to sit down with them in a neutral environment and outline exactly what you expect of them and what they can expect of you while at work.

They must be very clear that they can expect no favouritism because of their status as a friend as it would undermine both your and their integrity.

If you don't do this, it can become 'mission impossible' to maintain your integrity and to keep your department delivering the goods. This will not be easy, but as I stated earlier, if this results in the breakdown of your friendship, then maybe it wasn't such a good friendship after all.

The same advice above applies to family members you might be working with. Only, here you might have to be more tactful on how you deal with them, but ultimately, the same rules apply.

23 Managing Up

Everybody has a manager. You have a manager, your manager has a manager, even the MD or CEO of an organisation has a manager in the board of directors and indeed, they have a manager which would be the shareholders. So, everyone is subject to both managing people and being managed by people.

As you well know, it's one thing to manage people, but an entirely different matter being managed by someone.

There are good, bad and indifferent managers, trusting macro-managers and distrusting micro-managers and a whole variety in between.

Your manager is supposed to be there to support you, but what if they don't?

Managing your manager can be a tricky and difficult thing to do, but if you don't, you might get overridden, badly treated, taken advantage of and made the scapegoat for all your managers' indiscretions.

People are naturally ambitious (so are you, that's why you are a manager or an aspiring manager). Consequently with ambition can come ethical misbehavior. Not everyone is like this (I presume you are not), but when you are faced with an ambitious manager, you are going to have to manage them effectively or you could get trampled.

- Communication is the most important thing in any relationship including that between you and your manager. I have had a manager who simply refused to communicate with me. We went through one dry spell of four and a half months without a word spoken, phone call, e-mail or anything. This admittedly was a difficult one. You have to keep the communication channels open at all times. Even if you do not get a response, maintain the moral high-ground by keep your manager informed, even if it is only by e-mail. By communicating via e-mail you build up a record of your efforts should you need to provide some proof of this at some stage.

- Consistent delivery is critical. No matter what your relationship is with your manager, you must deliver consistently against your job profile, against your KPI's & KPA's both personal and for your department. Ensure that all reports are submitted on time and all deadlines are met. Keep your nose clean and make sure that no finger can be pointed at you for any lapse or failure. This is your foundation. This is what you will build your manger's trust on and enhance your reputation amongst your peers and colleagues and indeed, amongst your seniors. It is when they see that despite difficult or adverse conditions of work and a strained relationship with your manager, you never faltered at producing the goods!

- Know your rights within your job profile and the organisations policies. This will allow you to withstand being pushed around or having every meaningless job and task dumped on your desk. The difficulty here is to be able to stand up for your rights. You do this through being humble but firm, "I'm sorry sir, I will not be able to do this with the rest of my work load!' or "I'm sorry sir, this does not fall within my profile and in fact belongs to so and so or to that department'.

If your manager forces you to do it by saying 'You will do it, I am instructing you to do it!' or through coercion or threat, 'Are you refusing to obey a legal and lawful instruction?' or 'I will take disciplinary action against you or I will fire you' etc. then you need to do it, but first send him and e-mail wherein you outline the problem, his requirement, your response, his coercion or threat, your acquiescence and the potential consequences of you doing the task. This is called a diaper move or CYA (Cover Your Arse). Should things go pear shaped, you have in writing your objections to having to carry out his instructions and this could be your defense in a disciplinary action.

- Gather evidence. In any job, if you do not know your rights, then you are only as safe as your manager likes your face. If you feel at risk, or are not satisfied with your treatment or have a dysfunctional relationship with your manager, you need to be prepared for any eventuality. Facts are what wins the day, so, e-mails, memo's, reports or anything in writing either received by you, and/or sent or responded to by you are what you need to gather. It goes back to one of my other points, 'If it is not in writing it never happened'. It is imperative that any telephonic or verbal conversation you have with your manager that is a problem is responded to with an e-mail to establish the facts. You can start the mail with 'As per our conversation/ telephone conversation at 09h30 this morning

(12.07.15) for clarification purposes...' Then you outline the conversation, with the manager's requirements statements threats etc. your responses and the final conclusion. Other evidence can be reports that you made, Power Point Presentations etc. You can send copies of all this to your private mail, but beware, this can be against company policy and if so, do not do it. In addition, if you are trying to maintain a low profile, e-mail trails are easily traceable. The alternative is to print hard copies and file them in a safe place in your office, or take the copies home. Remember, you have the right to be treated fairly and to defend yourself.

- Having looked at various defensive techniques to protect yourself with, we must also look at the pro-active techniques that can and should be employed. It is always better to work within a positive framework and state of mind than in a defensive and negative one.
- You must try and keep positive dialogue with your manager, even if he is a grumpy old octogenarian who should have retired 30 years ago. To do this you have to look at the positives. Should he/she give you an instruction which turns out to be something smart, then try sending a very brief mail to your manager simply stating 'I have done as you requested. It has worked well. Thank you as I have learned something new today'. A little note like this can go a long way to breaking down barriers as it will garner a feeling of satisfaction and achievement within your manager and they might start looking at you from a different perspective. Do not flood you manager with hundreds of rubbish emails expounding their glories and wisdom as it will have the opposite effect. Nobody likes

someone who sucks-up unless they have an inferiority complex.

- Have confidence. Bullies are cowered by people who stand up to them and who exude confidence. If you come to your manager in a confident manner, they will learn to accept you for who you are. Stand up straight, keep your feet firmly on the floor, do not shuffle, keep your hands still, do not wring them, keep your head up, chin up and look them directly in the eye. Be careful not to come across as aggressive or arrogant, this will work against you.
- Greet them daily in a friendly manner and say goodbye to them daily in a friendly manner, even if they do not respond. One day they will start responding. Keep the greeting short and simple. Do not enquire after their health, family, children, dog etc. Nobody wants to answer a lot of questions to someone on issues that are private and have nothing to do with them.
- Engage the assistance of Human Resources (HR) if necessary. This however must be done with great caution. HR managers find themselves in a very precarious position within a company as they have to both ensure the company operates within the dictates of the law and company policies and provide support to those driving the company. Sometimes this can create a conflict of interest. Say for instance you are a junior manager and your problem manager is well like amongst his peers. They all know he is hard on his team, but he gets the result. Where do you think the weight of propensity will lie when you place this with the HR manager? Whilst trying to remain neutral, they will have to take sides invariably against you, for to side

against management could be a career limiting move for them. They are also only human and subject to the same pressures you are.

- Even the nice managers need to be managed. This is through communication, delivery, and support. They are easier to talk to and more willing to share. See if you can find common ground such as a rugby or soccer team you both support, or golf, your pets, outdoor activities, anything. The moment you have established common ground with anyone, it is that much more difficult for them to dislike you.

- Lastly, learn. Learn from your manager on how to manage people or how not to manage people. Learn what techniques they employ and how those techniques pushed your buttons either in a good or a bad way.

Irrespective of whether you have a good, bad or indifferent manager, ultimately they are still your manager and you need to respect them. If you can't respect the person, then at least respect the position.

24 Listen

Listening is probably the most flawed and underutilised sense in humanity today. Nobody listens; everybody has an opinion and believes that they must expound it. It is imperative to get up on your soap box and say your piece. I have a friend who always says, "Every arsehole has an opinion!"

The most infuriating thing to me is to be in a meeting, or a conversation where everyone is so busy expounding their opinion that two or three people are talking at the same time and nobody is listening to what the other person has to say. I make it a point of courteously giving someone the opportunity to say their piece. I then expect them to keep quiet and listen to what I have to say.

I have a rule, I never indulge in an argument. In an argument, both parties are trying to force their opinion on the other, neither listens to what the other has to say. It's a complete waste of time, emotion and breath.

The rudest and most unprofessional thing you can do is not listen to someone when they have something to say to you. This is particularly pertinent when dealing with your staff. They have a right to be heard and you as their leader have an obligation to listen.

Listening is an art. It is one of the more difficult things to learn to do properly. Natural human inclination is to listen to the first part of what someone is saying and then to start formulating an answer.

If you find yourself starting an answer with the word 'but', stop yourself for it means you have not listened. When in conversation with someone and they start a response, or start interjecting with 'but' I know they have not listened to me and I will often simply terminate the conversation at that point.

So how do you become a good listener? There are a number of listening techniques you might employ:

- Stop doing whatever you are doing immediately and turn your full attention to the speaker.
- Look them in the eye and patiently wait for them to finish what they are saying.
- Take time to reflect on what it is that they have said before you respond so that you can give full consideration to what they have said and so that they know you are doing so.
- Do not fidget, look at you watch, glance at you phone or computer screen or look out of the window. Give them your full attention.
- Pay attention to what they are saying. This can be difficult if the person is bashful, nervous or not speaking in their mother tongue. The second you lose focus on what is being said, your eyes will reflect it and the speaker will know you are not paying attention.
- Ask leading questions to gain clarity or to help them express themselves if they are speaking in their second or third language.
- Have patience.

- Do not jump to conclusions.
- Do not attempt to finish their sentence even if you think you are being helpful.
- Attune your ear to their accent and make allowance for poor grammatical construction of their sentences.
- If possible, change to their mother tongue to make it easier for them.
- Practice these techniques consciously for they do not come easily.

Most parents will make the effort to listen to their children (you should be if you are not doing so now). Your staff are your family at work. You in all probability spend more time with them than your own family, so therefore you should be giving them the same attention you would your own family.

Always listen carefully, give due consideration to what is being said and answer fully, clearly and honestly.

Heed the words of rock legend Jimi Hendrix where he says "Knowledge speaks, but wisdom listens!"

Work Ethic:

"Responsibility is a unique concept... You may share it with others, but your portion is not diminished. You may delegate it, but it is still with you... If responsibility is rightfully yours, no evasion, or ignorance or passing the blame can shift the burden to someone else."

Admiral Hyman G. Rickover

25 If it's not in Writing, it Never Happened

Every instruction must be in writing, every conversation must be followed up in writing, CYA.

How many times in the past have you said, or heard someone saying "I have told him/her so many times to do it this way", or "not to do that" and they just don't listen.

Alternately, how many times have you been faced with the situation when something has not been done, or some instruction not carried out, and the person says "You didn't tell me to do it" or "I don't recall being asked to do that" or "That's not how I understood what you said" and you don't have a leg to stand on because it is your word against their word. The person could be the office 'problem child' who knows how to play you and the system, or it could be a staff member who simply forgot and really can't remember you telling them.

Being faced with this situation can be very frustrating, embarrassing and indeed career limiting in some instances. It's the old classic of being caught with your pants down. Every manager will be faced with this problem sometime in their career.

My staff in the various companies I have worked for have gotten to know that should they come to me with a complaint, or if they are attempting to explain a breakdown in instructions given to someone and I ask 'Did you follow-up in writing" and they say' No!', I will simply tell them that it never happened. This applies to you too. If you fail to issue an instruction in writing, or if you fail to follow up a conversation with agreements in writing outlining clearly the instruction or the conversation and agreement, how can you go back to that person and query any aspect of it. If you don't have proof or record of what was instructed or what was discussed and agreed too, it becomes a matter of their word against yours for any deviation or failure that might have arisen.

It is also grossly unfair to issue your team members with a set of instructions and expect them to remember everything you said and also interpret what you were thinking behind the instruction without giving them a back-up set of instruction in writing. The human mind is fallible and so is human memory. Do not put it to the test and expect exemplary results, you will be disappointed.

If anything goes wrong, ultimately as manager, you are to blame, you should have known better. You should have followed up in writing.

Cover Your Ass (CYA). If you fail to cover it in writing, then don't cry when you get your butt kicked!

26 If it doesn't look Right, it isn't, Fix it.

This means exactly what it says. I have this maxim posted on the entrance door to my warehouse and on every notice board in my facility.

If you walk through the warehouse or stockyard, or office and something is out of place, it just doesn't look right or should not be there, then there is a problem. Have it attended to immediately. Do it yourself if necessary. Do not delay, set the standard for your team to follow, now is the time, for later could be too late. Companies with high standards of HSE such as the petrochemicals industry and foods manufacturing industry know that safety is the number one requirement for every staff member at all times. Safety can never be compromised under any circumstances. If something is not safe, it must be fixed immediately and it is your responsibility to ensure that it is done.

We all suffer from 'Industrial Blindness' from time to time. So what is industrial blindness you may be asking? It is the practice where through regular exposure you stop noticing things. This could be dirty marks on the walls, staff not wearing Personal Protective Equipment (PPE), items left in a dangerous or exposed place or boxes of files mounting up in the office. Because you see it every day, you stop noticing it. It is your job as manager to be aware of this and to look to the details of everything at all times so that when you see that it is not right, you can fix it.

The standards imposed in your locus of control are a reflection of your personality and your team will pick this up and mimic you. If you choose to overlook something or ignore a hygiene or safety issue, so will your staff as they will follow your example. You need to lead by example, set the standard and be the eyes and ears of everybody on your team. Importantly, do not procrastinate for procrastination is the thief of time and the roadway to ruin. Successful managers and leaders are people who seem to get everything done. Why is this you may ask? It is simple, they never procrastinate and they act on anything that comes to their attention immediately.

Don't be shy to make use of technology to assist you. Smart phones, tablets etc. are now standard operating tools. Take photos of problem areas you have identified and e-mail them to the responsible person for action, make notes on your device of what needs attention and when you get to your office follow through with the required team members by e-mail for attention. Why you might ask do I keep on saying" by e-mail'? Its quiet simple, if it is not in writing it never happened!

I use the camera on my mobile phone to take photos of anything I see that is amiss so that I don't have to try and remember it or write it down. It makes life very easy.

In this day and age of high pressure working environments, lean teams, advanced technology, intense customer competition and ever tightening deadlines, it is easy for something to slip your mind, or appear less important than something else and get forgotten. Managers and leaders are not infallible; indeed, we are as fallible as the next person. So how do you manage this? You do it through prompt and immediate action.

If it doesn't look right, it isn't, fix it – Now!!!

27 If it's Worth Doing its Worth Measuring

If it's worth doing, it's worth measuring; conversely, if it's not worth measuring, it's probably not worth doing. I am dyslexic and mathematics is not my forte. To this day I am unable to grasp algebra and don't see the sense in it. At school I was hopeless at accountancy and was thrown out of the class after two terms. I gave up maths completely at high school as I had not passed a math's test or exam in the eight years I had been at school. I hated anything mathematical (and still do today) and avoided it like the plague. Yet, I excelled at technical drawing for woodwork and passed my exams on Financial Management and Decision Making and Corporate Finance for my MBA. I often pondered this and came to realise that when working with figures that had a purpose and meaning to them, I enjoyed it. As I advance in my career into management I became more involved in KPI's, budgets and a variety of 'work' related calculations.

I came to realise that management is a mathematical art. Everything needs to be calculated and quantified whether it is staffing levels, budgets, performance measurement, production, scheduling, operational or fleet costs. Everything you do as a manager has a mathematical implication attached to it. 'Not true!' you say, 'there is no mathematics in staff motivation, management or discipline!' Wrong!!!

Whether it is disciplining or motivating or training staff, time is involved, time costs money, operational and work impact is involved and this costs money. Covering of absent staff requires rescheduling of staff (maths), salary differentiation between the absentee and coverer (maths), performance output of absentee verses coverer (maths), cost to company in productivity (maths), your personal time and that of others dealing with the discipline/training in terms of time value (maths). And so on and so forth.

So where are we heading with this? Every action or activity has a measurement. Every measurement has a cost tied to it. Everything one does can be broken down into pounds and pence, or dollars and pennies. This is the basic essence of Activity Based Costing. This is the bottom line cost!

But this is not exactly what I want to discuss.

The key to efficiency is to manage activity and thus manage cost. If every activity has a cost, then it is imperative that you determine what is worth doing and justifying the cost and what is not worth the cost so not worth doing. To determine this, you have to measure! This will allow you to prioritise activities, eliminate waste and manage costs. If an activity is worth the cost of doing, then it is worth measuring in order to determine what that cost is so that you can eliminate waste and control cost.

If you believe that some activity is not worth measuring, then it is probably not worth doing as it is costing money that you now can't account for and could be better employed elsewhere.

Many businesses have activities that add cost but little value as they are generally a 'nice to have'. Many businesses have extensive measurement of every activity they do, but never evaluate the information to determine the impact and value of the activity. The people employed to manage these recording activities are in themselves a non-value adding cost, but the reams of data look good so nobody questions it.

As a manager, it is your responsibility to evaluate the activities you do to determine the most cost effective way of doing it. You need to measure the activities to determine that cost.

Further to this, you need to evaluate what all you are measuring and why, do you use the information, does it add value? You need to determine whether it is worth the cost of someone's time and the company's resources to measure it and if it is not, eliminate it.

If it is worth doing, measure it and manage it, if it simply costs money and adds no value, eliminate it. You will find by eliminating activities and measurement that do not add value, you department or operation will be more efficient. Your staff will be more productive as they are not wasting their time and energy on valueless activities and ultimately, you will find the cost to operate you department, business or operation comes down.

By measuring all activities to determine the value-add and the benefits, you will ensure that you operation becomes more efficient. If your operation is more efficient, then both you and your staff will in effect be working smarter and not harder. This will reduce stress and pressure and be beneficial to the wellbeing of your staff. If your team is happy and contented then their out-put will be higher and as a consequence, your cost will be lower.

What does all this mean, you might ask? Well it is simple, by measuring and understanding all your activities, you know what is going on in your department. Your reputation as an efficient and effective manager will be enhanced and your career will benefit thus fitting in with 'the reason why you are doing all this'. You will be able to impart your learning upon your team so they will become more efficient in what they do and hopefully it should benefit their career as well, which fits in with 'Sharing the Wealth' and garnering the loyalty of your staff – even though you have a dog!

So when in doubt, measure it!

28 Money Talks and Bullshit Walks

A bit rude you may say! Indeed it is, but it very succinctly emphasises the point.

Benjamin Franklin, one of the founding fathers and the 6th president of the United States of America said "Well done is better than well said!" This advice is just as pertinent today as it was in the 1700's.

Don't tell me how good you are or how well you can do the job – show me!

Likewise, don't tell people how good you are and how well you can do the job – show them!

I have encountered numerous people in my travels, subordinates, peers and indeed senior people who were fantastic orators on their abilities but failed miserably when it came to delivery. If you cannot 'walk the talk', then don't talk. If you want to impress, keep silent and deliver the goods.

Bob Dylan says it best where he states "You can fool some of the people all of the time, and all of the people some of the time, but you can't fool all of the people all of the time".

There is nothing that impresses more than delivery and results. The key however to this delivery is accurate, complete, consistent total delivery. Do a half-job or take a short-cut at your own peril. This is a two-way street, it applies equally to you as it does to anyone you might deal with or manage.

You can embellish and fabricate all you want, but remember; bull-shit gives of its own smell and sooner or later you will be caught out.

This applies to your team as well, you will always have staff who can talk a good game but are not so hot on delivery. Learn to evaluate your team on their personal strengths and weaknesses so that you can assign jobs accordingly and assess delivery accurately. The key to delivery is personal KPI's for each team member. Regular evaluation will keep them on track and highlight any short-fall or excellence. Don't let your team members tell you how good they are, make them put their money where their mouth is.

This is also important when interviewing people for a position, particularly new people. Don't just let them tell you how good they are at the job, ask for examples to demonstrate their abilities and then test their answers with probing questions. When interviewing new staff, my standard question is "Give me an example of; i.e. how you do this task, or handle such a person, or evaluate this data etc." Someone who is honest will be able to give clear examples whereas a chancer will prevaricate and try to talk around the question.

Stand and deliver, promises are just so much hot air.

29 Bullshit Baffles Brains, but the Facts Baffle Bullshit

Also a bit rude, but indeed, so true.

If you can't back up your claims with facts then you will be blown out of the water.

In any situation be it financial reporting, KPI presentation arguing a proposal, motivating a team member or dealing with a disciplinary incident, if you do not have facts to back up your argument, you have nothing but bluster. The most powerful tool in your management arsenal is facts.

Facts form the basis on which you operate. Facts can back up your claims and prove your case. Facts are the building blocks to succeeding. Facts substantiated mathematically are the strongest.

There can be a down side to facts however. This down side is when you only know some of the facts not all of them. When you are unable to collate the facts into logical order to support your argument, or when you present the facts in a jumbled manner that confuses your audience, it creates opportunity for them to isolate the facts and tear them apart.

You need to see yourself as a soldier, the facts being your protective equipment, arms and ammunition. If you leave some of it behind, you have a problem, if you do not know how they work together, you have a problem, if you don't know where they fit in the greater order of things, you have a problem, if you don't know them well enough to use them correctly, you have a problem.

So in short, ensure that;

a) You have all the facts necessary
b) You know the facts thoroughly
c) You know where and when to use the facts
d) You know what facts must be presented in what sequence
e) You know what facts are ammunition and what facts are weapons.

Lastly, facts without figures are invariably unsubstantiated and therefore weak and hard to defend. If you have the facts but don't have the figures to support them, you place yourself at an extreme disadvantage.

If you have to do a presentation, submit a proposal, defend an action or deal with disciplinary matters, you must know the facts pertaining to your subject and when and how to use them.

Do your homework! If you do not have all the facts necessary, do not proceed.

30 Attention to Detail

Having an eye for attention to detail and effectively applying it will establish a reputation for you as someone who misses nothing, is focused on quality and will accept nothing less.

How do you do this?

It requires continual vigilance. When you walk through your operation, if something is not right, you identify it and have it corrected. If there is dust on the racking, or a single piece of trash or paper on the floor or if something is not packed, stacked or staged neatly you immediately identify it. If you have to read a document or a report, do it with focus not only on the message, but the construction and grammar of that message. Dot the i's and cross the t's. Read the small print. It is human nature not to want to read the small print, but this is extremely important, if you overlook a detail because it was too much effort to read the small print, it could come back to bite you. This is particularly important when you are reading or setting up contracts or Standard Operational Procedures.

Companies, particularly in the 80's and 90's liked to include in their small print 'An act of God'. I refuse to accept this statement because if you are religious you, are acknowledging that your God is a God of malicious destruction and disaster. Make the company change this to 'Force Majeure' it is less offensive and more encompassing. If you take care of the small details, invariably, the bigger issues will take care of themselves. In an operation, if you focus on the details such as HSE and hygiene, then it is more difficult for bigger things to go wrong if all the details have been adhered too. If you set the example in focusing on the details, you team will become acclimatised to focusing on them as well and the quality and standard of work will be higher. You cannot do a sloppy or untidy job if you are focusing on ensuring that the details are addressed because you are forced to think thoroughly on what you are doing and so it is more difficult to overlook something. There is an old expression I have heard numerous times over the years that states 'Take care of the details and the rest will take care of itself'.

I once applied for a job with a leading company is South Africa to manage a new distribution center they were opening. I was called to an interview at a hotel where the MD and the HR Director were staying on business. I was appropriately attired and had prepared well for the interview. When the interview commenced, I opened my briefcase and took out my note pad and opened it. I told them that I had 36 questions in five categories I wanted to ask them. The MD looked at me and said 'You have an eye for attention to detail!' I responded by saying that attention to detail is the foundation of management. I believe to this day that with his observation and my response I had already secured the job despite the fact that the interview had not officially started yet.

So, pay attention to detail in everything that you do. There is an old expression that says 'The devil is in the details!' Indeed, that is true. Be aware of that and be sure to pay attention to detail.

31 Plan and Prioritise

Work pressure is relentless and deadlines wait for no man.

How do you manage this pressure particularly if you have an onerous workload?

Have you ever looked at CEO's, MD's and Directors and wondered how they manage their workload? Yes, they have a secretary, but they do not lighten the workload, they only assist in organising it. They do it through prioritising what they have to do.

How does one prioritise?

I use a duel method. Firstly, I diarise what must be done against the date by when it must be done so that I can deal with things in the right order. Secondly, on a day to day basis I break my workload up into four categories by splitting the day in my diary into the following four sections;

- Things that must be done immediately
- Things that must be done immediately but can wait for the first batch of things to be done first
- Things of lesser importance that should be done on this day time allowing
- Things that can be carried over to tomorrow if necessary.

Indeed, it seems amateurish, but it works for me.

I then look at the low hanging fruit, things that can be done very quickly. By doing the things that can be done quickly first, you gain a sense of achievement and this gives you momentum to tackle the next task.

I use this strategy in each section starting with the things that must be done immediately and then work my way through each of the four categories.

If I am unable to complete all tasks on the day, the unfinished items get carried over to the next day but get moved up a category.

It is important to spend a short time at the end of each day planning for the next day. When you come in the next day, after doing your walk-about, do a quick review to include any new items that have cropped up.

As we all know, there is never enough time in the day to achieve all that must be done, that is why it is imperative to plan each day's activities and to prioritise them in order of importance. By doing this you will firstly not forget to do anything and secondly you will find that you can become very proficient in achieving all that you need to do.

The old expression of 'Failing to plan is planning to fail' is very true.

So, plan your day and prioritise your work.

"Either you run the day, or the day runs you!"
Jim Rohn – American entrepreneur and motivational speaker

32 Be Innovative

Richard Templar, author of The Rules of Management (a brilliant book, I recommend it) said "If you always do what you've always done, you will always get what you've always got!" Einstein said "To continually do the same thing and expect a different result is madness!"

As managers we are often faced with the dichotomy of the drive for continuous improvement against 'we do it this way because we've always done it like this'. How can one implement continuous improvement if you can't change the way things are done.

As a manager and a leader, you must continually evaluate how things are done and seek a better way to do them. You must think outside of the box and be prepared to try out new ideas.

Before going to your team to implement your latest epiphany, it is advisable to bring them together to discuss the new idea with them. You need to be able to clearly articulate what you wish to do and show the benefits of this new plan against the current method of doing things. Get you team to discuss the merits and de-merits of your proposal and to put forward their suggestions and objections. It is here where the office 'difficult child' will be of most value as they will probably look at the proposal from an angle that nobody else including yourself has looked at and ask questions that need to be discussed.

Do not let old habits and comfortable practices become a roadblock to new suggestions.

The world is advanced by innovative thinkers. As a leader it is expected of you to be innovative. Do your homework thoroughly on any new ideas and if it indicates that it will deliver the results then implement it.

Just a word of caution however, sometimes a good idea might give all the indications of being what is needed, but be prepared to test the new idea first and if it does not work, abandon it. Flogging a dead horse will achieve nothing but frustration and persistent failure.

Successful implementation of an innovative idea will go down well with your team and your superiors, particularly if there is a definitive cost savings and operational improvement.

33 If You want Loyalty, get a Dog

This falls into two categories, loyalty from your company to you and loyalty from you to your company.

So you have joined a company with a powerful brand name and a good reputation and are happy, but over time, things lose their glint and you wonder why. It is simple; you are working for an entity. You are a number within that entity and nothing much more. Companies will argue against this claim, but see how quickly you could end up being fired, retrenched, downsized, resized or sidelined. Companies speak about people being their 'best asset'. Assets are there for the company's use, abuse, depreciation and disposal, and you are just another asset. I am always annoyed and insulted when referred to as an asset because my individuality and humanity has been stripped away and replaced as an object with a number. Companies wax eloquently on this subject and often have wonderful and commendable initiatives for their staff, but when the chips are down, heads will roll and the company will revert to the letter of the employment contract in how to deal with you if things become difficult. You as the individual need to understand this.

If you are ambitious and wish to progress in life, you cannot do it in one company. There simply is insufficient scope for this in terms of availability of positions for you to progress into. You will have to wait for someone to be fired, promoted, resign, retire or die. You need to look after yourself. Take your career in hand, plot what you wish to achieve, put in some target dates and then look within your organisation to determine the likelihood of reaching the next position. If it is high, stay on, if it is low, you need to look outside of your organisation. Do not fool yourself that you are indispensible to the company, nobody is. If you should be run over by a bus tomorrow and die, the company will replace you and your job will go on as usual and quiet probably without any hitches. A company is a bucket and all the individuals working for the company make up the water in the bucket. Take out one drop (that would be you) and there is no difference made to the level of the water in the bucket. It does not leave a hole either; as soon as the drop is removed the gap is smoothed over.

Companies will advocate the need for employees to be loyal to the company, but that loyalty is not always reciprocal. You as the individual will sacrifice your time, family, health, holidays, nights, weekends and wellbeing for the company. You might even get recognized for this with a pat on the head or maybe a letter. It might even include financial benefits or promotion but it will not include employment guarantee.

The reality of the situation is that the first priority of any company is self preservation, then profit and payment to investors and shareholders. Unless you are one of the executives who can incorporate their job preservation with that of the companies' preservation, then you are vulnerable and face the same possibility of being the victim of downsizing, right sizing, restructuring, realigning, economic readjustment, rebranding, corporate aligning or whatever they wish to call it. Yes, no matter how much you have sacrificed for the company or how loyal you have been, if the economy falters, or your company is involved in a take-over, you could become a statistic. I know that this is sticking a finger in the eye of people at executive and director levels, but have a look at the history of corporate repositioning.

Do not confuse commitment and dedication with loyalty. You should always be fully committed and dedicated to your job and your company while you are employed by them. You expect your company to be consistent in the provision and payments of the emoluments you receive and therefore the company has a right to expect dedication, commitment and results for that emolument.

But, if you want loyalty, get a dog, it will stick with you through thick and thin when the company won't. If you want a career, then sometimes it is necessary to climb to success on the rungs of different companies.

And the same applies for companies, if they want loyalty, they should get a dog.

34 Sometimes it's Better to Ask for Forgiveness than Permission

This is some of the most controversial advice you might ever receive. It is a favorite ploy of what we consider 'risk takers'.

If you know it will work and is the best for the operation/ person/organisation, then just do it, the results will help justify the explanation when asked to account.

Everybody at some point in time will be or has been faced with the dilemma of needing to do something which they know will work and is the best solution for the problem at hand.

They also know that obtaining permission or authorisation to do so will be close to impossible because the person who has to give the permission simply does not understand the problem or the solution. Sometimes the solution you wish to apply to the problem is against company policy or procedure, possibly because the policy or procedure is out of date or out of touch with fast changing environments.

So, what do you do? Play it safe and have to spend some very difficult moments explaining why you never took the right decision without blaming you boss and creating even more trouble for yourself. Do you ask for permission knowing the result and then be in a position to blame your boss by saying 'I was not authorised to do so', knowing that you have missed an opportunity to do good and indeed curried your bosses' ill will for having made them look stupid. Or do you keep quiet, take the chance and do what you know will work and then manage the fall-out of a successful implementation which invariably is mild. You could also keep quiet, take the chance and end up fired if things go pear-shaped.

It is all about the level of risk you wish to take, the confidence you have in your actions and your confidence in being able to manage the fall-out after implementation.

This is a decision that should never be taken lightly as it could cost you your job and career or it could cost the company a great deal of money and damage to its reputation. You have to be more than one hundred percent sure of a positive outcome.

My advice here is this. If you feel so sure that what you wish to do is the correct route and the correct solution, then you must be able to motivate this to your superiors. You need to do so in writing or in a Power Point presentation if necessary, clearly defining the problem. You need to outline the current situation through a SWOT analysis. You need to clearly define your proposed solution including the fact that it might be against policy or procedure and why that is and motivate why you wish to take this course of action. This takes time and clear thinking. You then need to send the proposal to your manager and if possible other key individuals and be prepared to argue your case.

Having said that, I have circumvented this process and gone with my instinct on a number of occasions in my career without mishap.

Criteria to take into account when making such a decision are;

- it must be an emergency or very urgent thus negating the time required for the proposal route
- there must be risk of financial loss to the company or its reputation if no action is taken
- there must be propensity for good financial gain or savings to the company if the action is taken
- if it is a safety issue where risk to life and limb and property are at stake
- there must be no risk to any person, property or the company's reputation if action is taken
- there must be a pressing operational demand with long term ramifications if action is not taken

Ultimately, if you feel strongly enough and are prepared to risk your job and reputation for your conviction, then go for it. The risk is all yours; you must be prepared to live with the consequences.

Nothing ventured is nothing gained.

35 It is better to Declare than to be Caught

From time to time one is faced with a situation where something has gone wrong, you have made the incorrect decision or you have made a mistake or you have made a deliberate decision which is now a problem.

Nobody knows about this so what should you do?

You could cover it up and keep quiet, maybe nobody will ever know.

There is only one course of action in a situation like this — declare what has transpired.

Put it on the table warts and all for everyone to see. By doing this you will suffer some embarrassment and possibly negative response from your seniors or colleagues. But your integrity will remain intact. Your reputation for being open and honest will be enhanced and you can hold your head high knowing that there are no skeletons in the closet that could emerge and perhaps cost you your job.

It is far better to suffer some embarrassment and gain a reputation of someone who made a stupid decision than to gain the reputation of someone who is inherently dishonest, underhanded, untrustworthy and deceitful.

Furthermore, someone might give you some advice on the issue that helps you forgo doing it again or offers you advice on how to rectify the issue.

It is better to declare your faults or mistakes than to be caught out in a lie or deceitful action.

36 A Place for Everything and Everything in its Place

The most important thing in managing a warehouse, office, production environment or workshop is order.

Any operation of any kind must be neat, tidy and orderly. Offices must be neat tidy and orderly, so must the grounds outside be. Workshops must be neat tidy and orderly at all times. Even your desk and you computer must be neat tidy and orderly.

Why is this so important?

There are a number of reasons.

The first reason is Safety. An untidy working environment is an unsafe environment. If things are lying around or left where they ought not to be, they create a danger for people moving in that area. Slipping and tripping hazards or falling hazards could result in injuries or death and cost time and money. Your first priority is the safety of your staff. In any operational environment or workshop it is easy for someone to get injured by tripping over a broom lying around, trash on the floor or tools left carelessly on the floor. Items stacked unsafely at height could fall down and injure a picker or mechanic or office worker.

This leads into the second issue, hygiene. Hygiene is critical in avoiding dangerous conditions or an environment where vermin and disease can flourish. Cockroaches in the kitchen or canteen, rats and mice in the warehouse or birds nesting in the rafters and splashing bird paint all over can result in illness and injury amongst your staff. In many circumstances, this could lead to the health authorities fining your company or shutting it down.

Lost time due to illness and absenteeism with the related costs of down-time and replacement staff all contribute to the bottom-line

Thirdly, security can be impacted with stock and items getting lost or miss-placed, broken and then hidden away or theft. This can cost your company a lot in time, reputation and money when it comes to having to write-off items that were broken or tools and parts that were lost or have disappeared and to replace them with new ones. It can cost extraordinary large amounts of money through theft, particularly if security is lax and controls poor. Theft rings are quick to spring up and difficult to break.

Fourthly, warehouse or operational integrity is another factor. If stock is not received or binned correctly it can lead to stock expiring in the warehouse, customer orders not being fulfilled and of stock being written off. The company's reputation can suffer and customers can be lost. This type of mismanagement could cost you the manager your job.

It is therefore important to put controls in place and to enforce them vigorously and strictly to prevent the above problems from occurring. Every item in your work environment must have a place and that item when not physically in use must be returned to its rightful place.

This goes for brooms and cleaning equipment, workshop tools and equipment, material handling equipment such as pallet jacks, forklifts and reach trucks. Parking places should be assigned. Items in the kitchen and canteen should all have a place. All warehouses or storage areas should have a warehouse management system (WMS) and this must be strictly adhered too. Cyclical checks of the warehouse should be done daily and wall-to-wall stock (inventory) checks done monthly. The stationary storeroom should have assigned places for all items.

There is only one place for trash, in the trash bin. There is never an excuse for any trash to be lying around anywhere ever. It is simply not acceptable and non-negotiable, even during picking operations.

This leads to the office environment. Piles of papers stacked on desks are not acceptable. An untidy desk is a sign of an unorganized mind. You may scoff at this and claim to have a random access filing system on your desk, but you as the manager should be setting the example.

Even the filing within your PC or desk top should be structured and orderly. The golden rule is one minute retrievable. Any file, document, statistic file, page of paper or report should be retrievable within one minute. This goes for you and for every one of your team members. This includes filing systems of hard documents, hardcopies of SOP's, HSE documents, delivery documentation, receiving documents, invoices etc.

Everything must have a place and everything must be in its place.

I learned the value of this during my years in the military. Every vehicle had to have a loading plan. This loading plan had to be in minute detail to the point of where a can opener could be found. The object of this was that anyone should be able to take the loading plan and go to a specific vehicle in the pitch dark and locate a specific item i.e. a can opener. I was in a medical battalion and knowing exactly where to find medical items at high speed under extreme conditions day and night, dark or light was critical, for wasted seconds could easily result in the death of a critically wounded soldier.

'Well, a working environment is not the military!' you might argue. Indeed it isn't, but it makes no difference. If your staff have no discipline or you have no discipline, things in your operational areas of control can and will go wrong, things will get lost, stolen or broken and injuries or illness will occur, and if it does, it is your fault as the manager.

So lead by example, tidy up your electronic workstation, tidy up your desk and office and make sure that everything in your operation has a place and everything is in its place.

Attention to detail in applying these rules is important. If it isn't right, fix it!

37 Management of Meetings

What is the definition of a meeting? It is a place where hours are wasted taking minutes.

Meetings are the bane of our life. We spend too much of our time in meetings which add no value and nothing is achieved.

I have a few rules which I apply to meetings I am invited to:

- I will only attend a meeting where I feel I can contribute meaningfully. If I feel I can add no value, or my opinion will be expressed by someone else attending, I decline the invitation.
- If I start attending a series of meetings wherein no headway is being made by the third meeting, I stop attending.
- If the meeting is poorly managed and is a free-for-all, I stop attending.
- If a meeting is in another location other to where I work, I will try and attend via conference call.
- If the minutes produced are too cryptic or do not clearly cover the agenda items discussed and no allocation of tasks coming out of the meeting are clarified, I stop attending. This is because half of the next meeting will be wasted trying to determine where the last meeting left off and the current one should start and who was supposed to do what for this meeting.

I have found that the best way to achieve results in a meeting is to chair it yourself. This has a number of advantages. As chairman it allows you to:

- Set the agenda strictly to what should be discussed in the meeting.
- Manage the meeting strictly against the agenda and thus work your way through the agenda items sequentially and in order.
- Control the meeting by stopping any discussion that takes place not pertinent to the agenda item being discussed. It is far too easy for the agenda item to be usurped by someone bringing up an interesting point not related to the agenda item and distracting the meeting and re-directing it in the wrong direction.
- Manage the minutes to ensure they are accurate, to the point and clear. If this means taking minutes whilst you chair the meeting then do so. If as a manager you feel that you are not capable of managing the minutes yourself or that you as chairman are too important to take minutes, then maybe you should not be chairing the meeting in the first place.
- Should you have a scribe to take the minutes, you can control the discussion in order to enable the scribe sufficient time to accurately record the minutes.
- Allocate action items to appropriate people and set the deadlines by which delivery of that action item is expected.
- Ensure that the minutes are circulated to all attendees and identified recipients within 24 hours of conclusion of the meeting.

- Follow up regularly with individuals regarding action items that have been allocated to them.

Meetings have a variety of purposes but each meeting has a very specific function. This could be to discuss an urgent problem or it could be a regular monthly or weekly meeting to discuss KPI's or operational issues. Alternately, it could be to discuss strategy, planning the way forward or dealing with a crisis. Whatever the reason, it is important that the meeting has a set structure, set agenda, set time and time duration and an action items schedule.

In my experience people attend a meeting, get copies of the minutes and file them and then 30 minutes before the next meeting there is a mad scramble to see if they have any action items they should have attended to and if possible provide evidence of execution or come up with a brilliant excuse for having not done it.

I have developed a set of practices for meetings which ensure that I am always prepared for the meeting and can run the meeting in one hour or less. Any regular meeting exceeding an hour is a waste of everyone's time as people cannot always concentrate for that long, minds wonder and people lose track of what has been said.

These are my standard practices for regular or repetitive meetings:

- Create a matrix format meeting document that allows you to simply plug in new data or write in new information under the applicable box. The front page will be a list of names of attendees and a list of others for circulation. This allows you to record present and absent personnel. The last page is the 'Action Items' matrix which lists the task to be done, the name of the responsible person and the required date of completion. The pages in-between the first and last will be the various agenda items each in its own box. Keep the last box open for 'General' wherein all items discussed that need not be listed in the specific boxes can be recorded.

- Target who should attend and what information they need to contribute. Then also allow for junior staff members to attend as training.
- Plan and prepare carefully for each meeting so that when you go into it, you have all your ducks in a row and can proceed smoothly and without a hitch.
- By working off the minute's document, each item is addressed in sequence and it does not allow for digressive discussion on non applicable issues.
- Should anyone bring up an issue out of sequence, ask them to please bring it up in the appropriate section and move on.
- Notes can be made directly onto the minute's document or directly onto your laptop as you go thus updating the minutes as you work through the agenda.
- Meeting timings must be adhered to as strictly as possible. I like starting my meetings exactly on time but will allow a maximum of 5 minutes for latecomers If someone comes in late, I question them on their failure to be on time. It is extremely rude to waste a number of other people's time because you simply can't bother being on time.

- I do not allow mobile phones in a meeting, they must be left outside. If theft is a problem in your office complex, they must be switched off and be out of sight. There is no compromise on this issue.
- When allocating action items to individuals or teams, be very clear on what is required and ensure that the action item is clearly recorded on the action items matrix. If what you have recorded is unclear or ambiguous, then it is your fault as chairman if the task is not completed properly.
- After all agenda items have been dealt with, I always go around the table to each individual to see if they have any further input. This is where pertinent items not on the agenda can be raised and recorded under 'General'.
- I then go through each action item and check that the delegated parties are absolutely clear on what must be done and by when.
- Minutes are written up and finalised for distribution immediately after the meeting. Either do it yourself or ensure that the scribe does it.
- Minutes must be circulated to all recipients if possible on the same day the meeting was held, but no later than 24 hours later.
- I keep a hardcopy of all minutes on my desk and go through them on a daily basis to follow up on what must be done, who should be doing it and by when it should be done. I follow up directly with the individuals on a regular basis.

By applying and adhering to the above criteria, I have reduced the various meetings I chair to a simple easily manageable format allowing me to hold multiple meetings on the same day if necessary. I have also reduced the time of meetings from 90 minutes and more to between 20 and 40 minutes.

The matrix format for meetings can be adapted and modified in a couple of minutes to suit any meeting you might need to hold.

Some companies have a specific meeting format. If your company does, then you need to work within the required parameters.

Meetings are a tool. If you learn to manage and manipulate that tool properly, it will be of great assistance to you. If you don't, it can become one of the most burdensome and wasteful exercises of your management day.

Conclusion

The world is full of management gurus, motivational experts and learned luminaries who have enlightened the modern era with their knowledge, expertise and advice. I am none of these.

I am simply an everyday manager like you who has had to bite the bullet in tough times, wrestle with moral and ethical as well as operational dilemmas in a working environment. Like you I have had to motivate people while personally feeling in the dumps and keep on smiling when there was nothing to smile about. I have also seen promotion opportunities go to less deserving people and suffered under management discrimination.

I have enjoyed the pleasures of watching team members develop and blossom into highly functional professionals. I have had the immense and incalculable pleasure of having team members keep contact with me for decades after we had parted working ways, because of the respect they have for me and the positive influence I have had on their lives. To me, this is what it is all about.

I owe this to all the people I have worked for over the years, management and other. They have influenced the way that I think and have impacted on how I operate.

Whilst you can learn all you like from books and studies, only you can effectively evaluate the physical situation you find yourself in, in order to apply the appropriate solution.

Your foundation will be based on common sense, experience, the rules of engagement, the desire for fair-play, making the hard decisions and ultimately treating others the same way you would wish to be treated.

Ultimately, the big question is;

'How do you become a better manager or a better leader?'

You do it by first becoming a better person.

Printed in the United States
By Bookmasters